The Essence of
SUFISM

The Essence of
SUFISM
JOHN BALDOCK

CHARTWELL
BOOKS, INC.

Published by
CHARTWELL BOOKS, INC.
A Division of BOOK SALES, INC.
114 Northfield Avenue
Edison, New Jersey 08837

First published by Arcturus Publishing Limited

This edition published 2004

British Library Cataloguing-in-Publication Data: a catalogue
record for this book is available from the British Library

© Arcturus Publishing Limited
26/27 Bickels Yard, 151–153 Bermondsey Street, London SE1 3HA

ISBN 0-7858-1860-X

Printed in China

Contents

Introduction

The Sufis are noted for their stories, many of which feature a semi-mythical character known as Mulla Nasrudin. At times Nasrudin appears profoundly wise, at others he behaves like a madman. Like life, he is unpredictable. So are the stories about him, for they usually involve one or more unexpected twists. Idries Shah, author of many books on the Sufis and Sufism, relates the following example:

> One day the villagers thought they would play a joke on Nasrudin. As he was supposed to be a holy man of some indefinable sort, they went to him and asked him to preach a sermon in their mosque. He agreed.
>
> When the day came, Nasrudin mounted the pulpit and spoke:
>
> 'O people! Do you know what I am going to tell you?'
>
> 'No, we do not know,' they cried.
>
> 'Until you know, I cannot say. You are too ignorant to make a start on,' said the Mulla, overcome with indignation that such ignorant people should waste his time. He descended from the pulpit and went home.
>
> Slightly chagrined, a deputation went to his house again, and asked him to preach the following Friday, the day of prayer.
>
> Nasrudin started his sermon with the same question as before. This time the congregation answered, as one man:

'Yes, we know.'

'In that case,' said the Mulla, 'there is no need for me to detain you longer. You may go.' And he returned home.

Having been prevailed upon to preach for the third Friday in succession, he started his address as before:

'Do you know or do you not?'

The congregation was ready.

'Some of us do, and others do not.'

'Excellent,' said Nasrudin, 'then let those who know communicate their knowledge to those who do not.'

And he went home.

(Idries Shah, *The Exploits of the Incomparable Mulla Nasrudin*, 44)

At first glance the story may appear to be little more than a joke about Nasrudin turning the tables on some slow-witted villagers. However, it also tells us quite a lot about the Sufis, not least in the way that Nasrudin, the Sufi, is introduced into the story as 'a holy man of some indefinable sort'. That is how the villagers in the story see Nasrudin. They are unable to fit him into their normal definition of who or what a 'holy man' is and how, in their view at least, he should behave. That is the most obvious thing the story has to tell us about the Sufis: they do not conform to normal expectations of who or what a 'holy man' should be.

The story also has something to say about ourselves, because that is who the 'villagers' represent; or, rather, it comments on the way in which we have been conditioned to behave and think. In fact this is the subject of the eccentric Mulla's sermons, but perhaps, because he says so few words it would be more accurate to describe them as practical demonstrations. In one sense the story is a practical demonstration too, for it offers us an illustration of two entirely different ways of thinking and behaving: the one represented by Mulla Nasrudin and the other by the villagers. The difference between these two ways is perhaps less ambiguously illustrated in another story, this time from *The Conference of the Birds,* a classic of Sufi literature written about 800 years ago by Fariduddin Attar, a Sufi from Persia.

> A rich man was riding along a city street when he passed a poor old
> man, dressed in rags, sitting in a doorway. Not knowing him to be
> a Sufi, the rich man stopped his horse, looked down at the person
> he took to be a beggar, and asked: 'Who is the better of the two
> of us, me or you?'
>
> The old man replied, 'O you ignoramus! Your words are as
> hollow as your head. I know that Sufis do not normally sing their
> own praises, but, since you oblige me to do so, let me tell you that
> one Sufi is worth a thousand men like you. Your ignorance of the
> Way has made you the slave of your inflated ego. You have been
> harnessed by it and it has made an ass of you, because you do
> whatever it tells you to do. Whoever follows the Way of Truth
> learns how to master his ego, and rides it like an ass. Now, since I
> have mastered what has mastered you, it should be obvious which
> one is the better of us. You are in love with your lower self. It has
> lit the fires of desire in you, and you are being burned alive in their
> flames.'

The essential difference between the two ways is that with one of them our
thoughts and behaviour are governed by our ego or 'lower self': with the
other they are not. When we have learned to master our lower self, a
transformation of consciousness takes place and we are guided by our 'higher
self'. In the simplest of terms, a Sufi is someone who has mastered his or her
ego and attained a higher state of consciousness.

There is, of course, much more to it than that. How much more depends
on how far along the Sufi Path we are willing to travel. As the above stories
about Nasrudin and the rich man and the Sufi demonstrate, the Path is not just
an intellectual exercise. It is a practical path of transformation and fulfilment
which enables us to free ourselves from the veils of the ego, unite the inner
and outer worlds and discover the unified self within.

To use a favoured Sufi analogy: the goal of the Sufi Path is for the drop (the
individual self) to merge with the Ocean of Being from whence it came. This
is what happens to us at the moment of our physical death, which is why all
true spiritual traditions encourage us to make that transition consciously,
while we are still in the body. 'Die before you die,' say the Sufis. In other

words, to be a Sufi is to die to who we have been conditioned to think we are, so that we might become what we are capable of becoming.

> The path of Sufism is the elimination of any intermediaries between the individual and God. The goal is to act as an extension of God, not to be a barrier.
> (Sheikh Muzaffer Ozak, *Love is the Wine*, 1)

A Sufism without Islam?

Many readers may already have heard the Sufis defined as 'Islamic mystics', or Sufism described as the 'mystical heart of Islam'. There is also a Sufism that, in the present context, could perhaps be described as 'Western Sufism' – that is, a Sufism that does not require its adherents to practise the religion of Islam. Further, some Westerners are drawn to Sufism because of the insight and understanding they feel they gain from studying it and yet neither wish to go further down the Sufi Path nor have anything to do with Islam. Writing in the 1970s, long before the words 'spirituality' or 'New Age' had entered our everyday vocabulary, William Stoddart gave voice to certain concerns raised by these different approaches to Sufism.

> Sufism is the spirituality or mysticism of the religion of Islam. Mysticism makes its appearance as an inward dimension in every religion, and to attempt to separate the mystical element from the religion which is its outward support is an arbitrary act of violence which cannot but be fatal to the mysticism, or spiritual path, concerned. In the present century, however, the attempt to do precisely this has been made repeatedly, and time and time again we are offered a Vedanta (or a yoga) without Hinduism, or a Zen (or something purporting to be such) without Buddhism.
>
> In recent times nothing has suffered more from this vain procedure than Sufism: in a variety of forms and in many parts of the Western world we are now offered a Sufism without Islam! One might as well try to purvey human life without a human body!

To be sure, the body (though made in the image of God) is corruptible and mortal, while life is invisible and immortal. Nevertheless, as far as we in this world are concerned, it is only in the body that life finds its support and expression. So it is also in the case of mysticism and spirituality: this is the inward and supra-formal dimension, of which the respective religion is the outward or formal expression. One cannot be a Benedictine without being a Christian, or a Sufi without being a Muslim. There is no Sufism without Islam.
(William Stoddart, *Sufism,* 19)

The concerns expressed by William Stoddart may seem even more relevant now in the context of today's anarchic pick-'n'-mix spiritual hypermarket, which has blossomed as a result of the disillusionment of many people with institutionalized religion. As a consequence of this antipathy to religion there are people who want Sufism without Islam. Yet, in a very real sense, Sufism is inseparable from Islam. Shaykh Fadhlalla Haeri, a Sufi shaykh who has written many books on Sufism for Western readers, explains why:

Sufism and Islam cannot be separated, in the same way that higher consciousness or awakening cannot be separated from Islam. Islam is not an historical phenomenon that began 1,400 years ago. It is the timeless art of awakening by means of submission. Sufism is the heart of Islam. It is as ancient as the rise of human consciousness.
(Shaykh Fadhlalla Haeri, *The Elements of Sufism*)

'Islam is not an historical phenomenon . . . It is the timeless art of awakening by means of submission.' The Arabic word *islam* means 'submission', or to be more precise 'the surrender of one's whole being', to the Divine Unity, to the Oneness that is God. It is the surrender of the drop as it becomes one with the Ocean.

As many Western readers will be unfamiliar with the historical context from which Sufism emerged, it seems appropriate that this should be covered by the opening chapters of an introductory book on the Sufis. Part One of this book, therefore, concerns itself with the life of the Prophet Muhammad, the

Qur'an, the principal tenets of Islam, the historical emergence of Sufism and the Sufis' use of symbolism. Part One ends with a chronological compilation of the biographies of Sufis from Hasan of Basra (d.728) to Imam Ghazali (d.1111), illustrated with anecdotal stories and extracts from their writings and teachings. Part Two takes a prolonged look at the lives and writings of four Sufis from the classical period of Sufism – Fariduddin Attar (d.1220/9?), Ibn 'Arabi (d.1240), Jalaluddin Rumi (d.1273) and Shabistari (d.1320). The book concludes with an appendix containing The Most Beautiful Names (the Ninety-Nine Names of Allah, as used in the Sufi practice of *dhikr*) and a Glossary of Sufi terminology.

A word needs to be said about the Arabic and Persian languages, the languages most associated with the era of classical Sufism. Both of these languages are consonantal. That is, only the consonants (cnsnnts), the root of the word, are written down. Although the same consonants may form the root of several words, sometimes with seemingly unrelated meanings, the correct sense is evident to native speakers from the context and their knowledge of the language. Written English is very different in that it is fully vocalized – the vowels are an integral part of the written language. (We use a consonantal form of English for the sake of abbreviation, as might be seen on a London bus – as in KNSNGTN, or KNGS CRSS – or be used in a text message to a mobile phone.) When Arabic and Persian words are rendered into the Latin (or Roman) alphabet used for English, the vowels are added and at this point variations in English spelling appear, depending on which particular system of transliteration is favoured by the author. As yet there is no standard system.

Part One

Chapter One:

The Prophet Muhammad

The Period of Ignorance

Towards the beginning of the seventh century CE, the political and cultural landscape of both the Near and Middle East was dominated by two great empires. From its capital Constantinople (now Istanbul), the eastern Roman Empire controlled most of the shoreline of the Mediterranean as well as the lands at its eastern end. Further east lay the Persian Empire, with its capital Ctesiphon. In the early decades of the century, these two empires were at war with each other. Under Chosroes II, the Persians embarked on a conquest of the Roman eastern provinces. Their progress was swift: western Mesopotamia, Egypt, Syria, Armenia and part of Anatolia all fell within a few years, during which the Persians took Jerusalem and captured Christendom's most sacred relic, the Holy Cross. In 622 the Romans were strong enough to launch a counter-offensive and by 629 Heraclius I had reconquered the lands taken by the Persians. He also returned the Holy Cross to Jerusalem, symbolizing the triumph of Christianity over Zoroastrianism, a religious tradition already in decline. Heraclius then overhauled the civil and military administration of the Empire, and Greek rather than Roman was adopted as the official language. In recognition of these cultural changes, historians refer to the old eastern Roman Empire, from the reign of Heraclius onwards, as the Byzantine Empire, Byzantion having been the Greek name for Constantinople before Constantine made it his capital.

On the southern edge of these mighty empires lay a very different culture: that of the nomadic Arabic-speaking Bedouin tribes of the Arabian Peninsula. Each tribe was autonomous, but a number of shared values were common to them all: loyalty to the family, clan, or tribe; pride in the ancestral lineage; and a love of independence. Tribal leadership was sometimes inherited directly, but leaders could also be appointed by general consensus when they exhibited the necessary personal qualities. Social stability and cohesion were maintained by the loyalty of the tribes' members and, in return, the tribe's wealth and possessions were shared generously among them. On the bigger scale, the vendetta-like code of justice which operated between the tribes prevented any one tribe from obtaining dominance over the others. At the same time, the constant warfare between the tribes made it impossible for the Arab people to unite behind a common purpose and found a civilization of their own. This lack of unity was to some extent reflected in their religious beliefs.

In contrast to the monotheistic religions of the neighbouring Byzantine and Persian Empires the Arabs had a pantheon of pagan deities, Although they worshipped at the deities' shrines, the focal point of worship for the Arabs was the massive cube-shaped shrine of the Ka'ba, which stood at the heart of an ancient sanctuary (*haram*) in Mecca. Known as the Holy House or House of God, it was dedicated to *al-Lah,* the High God of the Arab pantheon. The Ka'ba was also the setting for an annual pilgrimage (*hajj*) lasting several days, during which hostilities between warring tribes were suspended as Arabs from all over the peninsula made their way to Mecca to perform the traditional rites and rituals. These included circling around the Ka'ba and touching the Black Stone set in one of its corners.

Before the seventh century had run its course this ancient sanctuary was to become the focal point for the emergent monotheistic religion of Islam, which, like Judaism and Christianity, traces its origins back to Abraham (*Ibrahim*). The Qur'an relates that the foundations of the Ka'ba were raised by Abraham and Ishmael (Qur'an 2:125ff), at the place where, in submission to God's command, Abraham had made ready to sacrifice Ishmael, his son by his bondwoman (slave) Hagar. In the biblical Book of Genesis, Abraham demonstrated his submission to the Will of God by preparing to sacrifice Isaac, his son by his wife Sarah (Genesis 22). Genesis also tells how, prior to the sacrifice of Isaac, Hagar and her son had been abandoned in the desert at Sarah's request. Abraham was displeased at this but God reassured him, saying that, like Isaac, Ishmael would become the father of a nation. The account of Hagar's wandering in the desert is similar in both holy books, and many of the rituals in the annual pilgrimage to Mecca commemorate events that occurred in the lives of Abraham, Hagar and Ishmael. But we have jumped ahead of ourselves by making the connection between Islam and the Ka'ba. It is time to return to Mecca as it was at the end of the pre-Islamic period; a time known to Muslims as *al-jahiliyyah* (the Period of Ignorance).

Mecca

The Early Years

Muhammad was born in Mecca in 570 CE into the Hashim clan of the Quraysh tribe. A few generations earlier, the Quraysh had abandoned their nomadic way of life to become guardians of the sanctuary and at the time of Muhammad's birth they were the most powerful and prestigious tribe in Mecca. They were also highly successful traders and had turned Mecca into one of the most important cities in Arabia. The trade route linking the Mediterranean with southern Arabia and the Indian Ocean passed close to the city. Caravans would make a detour to visit the holy site and the suspension of hostilities that coincided with the pilgrimage enabled the Arabs in Mecca to trade with one another in peace.

Orphaned at an early age – his father, 'Abdullah, had died before he was born, and his mother, Aminah, before he was six – the young Muhammad was brought up by his grandfather, 'Abd al-Mutallib. During the *hajj* 'Abd al-Mutallib provided food and water for the pilgrims. He was also responsible for the upkeep of the Well of Zamzam (from which Hagar had obtained water during her desert sojourn with Ishmael), and so the young Muhammad would have acquired an intimate knowledge of the religious beliefs of the pagan Arabs. While watching over the family's flocks in the hills around Mecca, he would also have grown accustomed to periods of solitude in the arid landscape of Arabia. When he was eight he went to live with his maternal uncle, Abu Talib, who, like Muhammad's grandfather, was connected with the religious rituals of the Meccan sanctuary. He was also a merchant, and when Muhammad was about twelve years old he began to take him on trading trips, sometimes lasting several months. As the years passed, Muhammad's impeccable conduct in business earned him a reputation for honesty and he became known as the Trusted One (*al-Amin*). While still a young man he entered the employment of Khadijah, a wealthy widow some fifteen years his senior, and looked after her trading interests. They were married when Muhammad was twenty-five and Khadijah was forty. Of their seven children only their daughter Fatimah survived beyond childhood.

The transition from nomadic poverty to sedentary affluence had not been easy for the Quraysh. Their new position brought with it a decadence in which traditional tribal values were replaced by the unbridled pursuit of worldly wealth. Within the tribe itself, each of the clans or family units fought each other for a share of the riches, a situation that contrasted strongly with the earlier ethos whereby the tribal wealth was shared equally amongst its members. This new state of affairs led to considerable inequalities between rich and poor, whereas previously the wealthier members of the tribe had seen it as their duty to care for the poor. This did not go unnoticed by Muhammad who, as a trader, had acquired a reputation for fair dealing. He saw it leading to the disintegration of both tribal and social structures.

'Recite!'

As the years passed, Muhammad took to meditating for long periods in a cave on Mount Hira, outside Mecca. It was there, during a retreat in the month of Ramadan in 610, when he was about forty years old, that he received his first revelation in the form of a dramatic visitation from the Archangel Gabriel (*Jibreel*). It was night and Muhammad was either asleep or in a deep meditative state when the angel came to him and commanded: 'Recite!' (*iqura!*) In reply, Muhammad protested: 'I am not a reciter.' (A 'reciter' (*kahin*) was someone who went into an ecstatic trance and claimed to utter prophetic oracles. Muhammad was protesting that he was *not* one of these people.) The angel took him in a powerful embrace, holding him ever tighter until both his breath and his strength had been squeezed from him. Then the angel released him and commanded: 'Recite!' Again Muhammad protested: 'I am not a reciter'. The angel took hold of him, embraced him hard a second time, released him when he was on the point of exhaustion and commanded: 'Recite!' Again he protested: 'I am not a reciter'. For a third time the angel took him in an overpowering embrace and commanded:

> Recite: In the name of your Lord who created – created man from
> a clot of blood!
> Recite: Your Lord is the Most Bountiful One, who by the pen taught
> man what he did not know!
> (Qur'an 96:1–5)

Muhammad, who is described as an *ummi,* an 'unlettered' (that is, illiterate) one, found himself reciting the Word of Allah. With the descent of the Qur'an (meaning 'Recitation') Muhammad's mission as Prophet and Messenger had begun. Islamic tradition holds that on that particular night the entire Qur'an descended into the spiritual heart of the Prophet. It was to take many more revelations, given during the remaining twenty-three years of the Prophet's life, for this 'vertical' descent to be transmitted 'horizontally' – that is, for the entire Qur'an to be expressed in physical words. We shall be turning to the Qur'an in greater detail in the next chapter. For now we stay with the night the Qur'an was received, known as the Night of Power (*laylat al-qadr*), when the angels and spirits descended:

> Lo! We revealed it on the Night of Power (*Qadr*).
> Ah, what will convey unto thee what the Night of Power is!
> The Night of Power is better than a thousand months.
> On that night the angels and the Spirit descend, by the permission
> of their Lord, with His decrees.
> That night is peace, till break of dawn.
> (Qur'an 97:1–5)

The Night of Power was not Muhammad's first encounter with the Archangel Gabriel. Prior to his mother's death, he had experienced what is known as the 'Splitting Open of the Breast' (*shaqq as-sadr*) or 'Breast Washing'. On this occasion Gabriel had seized him and pushed him to the ground. His breast was split open, his heart removed and purified of a dark substance in it. After the purification of the heart, the Archangel replaced it, healed the Prophet's breast and went on his way. According to tradition, a similar experience occurred at other times in his life. In his book *The Islamic Tradition*, Professor Victor Danner explains the esoteric significance of this event:

> Symbolically, the event points to the removal of ignorance, represented by the dark substance, through the intervention of supernatural purification. The result is an unveiled or purified heart, source of impeccant [infallible] conduct thereafter. The celestial agent in the story is Gabriel – or, in other accounts, angelic beings – who blot out the transmitted legacy of the Fall. There is something prototypal in the whole sequence of events: mystical rebirth is implied therein. Muhammad's inward, celestial and chosen nature makes his outward, human nature conform to this primordial purity by removing all obstacles to its radiance. In the process, the resulting impeccance (*'ismah*) of the *rasul* [meaning 'Messenger'] is a lesson to the believer of mystical bent that he, too, must restore in himself the Edenic image through the elimination of the darkened clouds that cover the inner eye of the heart.
>
> (Victor Danner, *The Islamic Tradition*, 41)

In this passage Professor Danner mentions several themes to which we will be returning later: ignorance, a purified heart, the relationship between inner and outer natures and the eye of the heart. The imagery associated with the heart is of particular significance, for the Way of the Sufi is often referred to as the 'Way of the Heart'. Sufis also talk of 'polishing the heart'. This is not so that they can see themselves in it more clearly! Rather, polishing the heart signifies the erasure of the image of the individual 'self' which covers the eye of the heart like a veil. A polished heart reflects nothing but God. The veiling of the heart is an example of *ghaflah* (forgetfulness). Its opposite is *dhikr* (recollection or remembrance of God), the practice of which is the most effective way to polish the heart.

An essential part of Muhammad's message concerned another type of purification, the purification of the Ka'ba of its pagan idols, for Allah commanded: 'Purify My House' (Qur'an 2:125). With the removal of the idols from the sanctuary, the Ka'ba would return to the purpose for which it was intended: the worship of Allah alone. In other words, polytheism (*shirk*) would give way to monotheism (*tawhid*). But whereas our Western understanding of 'polytheism' (*poly*, 'many'; *theos*, 'god') and 'monotheism' tends to be in the narrow sense of 'many gods' and 'one God', the sense implied by the words *shirk* and *tawhid* is rather different.

To quote Professor Danner again: '*Tawhid* ("Divine Unity") . . . is the recognition that the Divinity, *Allah*, is the One who has no second, no associate, no parents, no offspring, no peers.' (Danner, *The Islamic Tradition*, 4) *Shirk*, the opposite of *tawhid*, is to attribute to any being or thing an existence that is outside or independent of the Divine Unity. As Allah asks in the Qur'an, 'Have you seen those who made gods of their own passions?' (25:43). In this regard, the decadent lifestyle and sense of self-sufficiency (*istaqa*) exhibited by the wealthier members of the Quraysh was tantamount to a declaration of independence from Allah. The early *Suwar* (singular *Surah* or Chapter) of the Qur'an are a reminder of Allah's benevolence. As Karen Armstrong, the writer and broadcaster, says:

> The Qur'an was not teaching the Quraysh anything new. Indeed, it constantly claims to be 'a reminder' of things known already, which it throws into more lucid relief. Frequently the Qur'an introduces a topic with a phrase like: 'Have you not seen . . . ?' or 'Have you not considered . . . ?' The Word of God was not issuing arbitrary commands from on high but was entering into dialogue with the Quraysh. It reminds them, for example, that the Ka'ba, the House of al-Lah, accounted in large measure for their success, which was really in some sense owing to God. The Quraysh loved to make the ritual circumambulations around the shrine but when they put themselves and their own material success at the centre of their lives they had forgotten the meaning of these ancient rites of orientation. They should look at the 'signs' (*ayat*) of God's goodness and power in the natural world. If they failed to reproduce God's benevolence in their own society, they would be

out of touch with the true nature of things.
(Karen Armstrong, *A History of God*, 166)

'Orientation' is a key word here, for it means more than simply pointing oneself physically in a particular direction. It also refers to our inner orientation, whether this is towards ourselves – that is, to our ego-personality – or towards something much greater, to the Source on which we depend for our being. Orientation towards the latter entails an act of submission, the surrender (*islam*) of our whole being to the Divine Will. (A person who surrenders his or her whole being in this way – that is, practises *islam* – is a *muslim*.) Without this total surrender we remain oriented towards our ego-personality, and subject to its every whim and desire. From a certain point of view, however, there is no separation between what we refer to as our 'inner' and 'outer' lives. Our outer life corresponds to our inner state. For this reason the ritual prayers (*salat*) instigated by Muhammad involved the physical act of bowing down, an outer gesture which both confirmed and would help to develop the inner orientation.

Knowing that his message would not go down well with the proud Quraysh, Muhammad refrained from preaching publicly for a period of about three years. Instead he delivered his message in private. Those who accepted his Prophethood in these early years were few. Tradition relates that Khadijah, his loyal and supportive wife, was the first, followed by 'Ali, his cousin. Others began to follow in increasingly large numbers.

When Muhammad's teaching first came to the attention of the Quraysh they did not object, thinking it to be just another money-making cult to add to the many already using the Ka'ba and the sanctuary. All this changed in 613 when Muhammad began preaching publicly. He called upon the Meccans to reject the many different pagan religions, to remove the idols from the Ka'ba and to surrender to Allah, the One and Only God, the God of Abraham and all the Prophets. In so doing he not only challenged the position of power and wealth enjoyed by the Quraysh as guardians of the sanctuary, but he also threatened to undermine part of the traditional way of life of the Arab people.

The response of the Quraysh was predictably hostile. Why should they give up their wealth and prestige? Yet by preaching a return to the religion of Abraham, Muhammad continued to gain the acceptance of his teaching, especially among the smaller clans. The situation came to a head in 616, when Muhammad used his position as one of the guardians of the Ka'ba to deliver his message to the wider audience of pagan tribesmen, who came from all over Arabia to worship in the sanctuary. Some of the elders of Muhammad's clan, the Hashim, now turned against him because of a boycott imposed on their merchants by the other clans of the Quraysh. As hostility increased, some seventy or so of Muhammad's followers fled to Abyssinia, where they sought the protection of Negus, the Christian ruler.

The Night Journey (Isra') *and Ascent* (Mi'raj)

One evening Muhammad was by the Ka'ba, 'in a state between sleeping and waking', when Gabriel (*Jibreel*) appeared to him and told him to mount a winged beast called Buraq. The animal, which was 'smaller than a mule and larger than an ass', had a woman's head and a peacock's tail. Muhammad's wondrous steed took him to Jerusalem, to the site of the ruined Temple of Solomon, where Abraham (*Ibrahim*), Moses (*Musa*), Jesus (*Isa*) and all the other Prophets were gathered. Muhammad led them in prayer, and then Buraq bore him upward to the Seventh Heaven. As they passed through each of the seven heavens he met one or another of the Prophets who had preached the Oneness of God to humankind.

While in Heaven, the Voice of Allah informed Muhammad about the obligatory prayers he and his followers would be required to perform. On his way out he passed Moses, who asked him about the prayers. Muhammad told him that Allah had commanded them to pray fifty times a day. Moses suggested that this was too heavy a burden and counselled Muhammad to beg Allah to reduce it. His request was granted and it was established that the obligatory prayers were to be repeated five times a day (a figure that coincides with the number of our physical senses). Buraq then carried Muhammad back to Mecca that same night.

The Night Journey from Mecca to Jerusalem (*al-isra'*) and Muhammad's Ascent (*al-mi'raj*), which are described in the Qur'an (Surah 17) and many Prophetic Traditions, are of key importance in the Islamic tradition: they are commemorated in the annual festival of the Night of Ascent (*laylat al-miraj*). The site on the Temple Mount in Jerusalem from which Muhammad ascended to Heaven is marked by the Dome of the Rock, Islam's most holy shrine outside Mecca. (Built c.691, some sixty years after the death of Muhammad, it is one of the first and purest examples of Islamic architecture.) The esoteric teaching associated with the *isra'* and *mi'raj* is explained by Professor Danner:

> The movement horizontally from Mecca to Jerusalem at night has relations with the self-extinction, 'the dark night of the soul', that proceeds the upward, vertical ascension of the Spirit. Indeed, the descent (*tanzil*, which also means 'revelation') of the Qur'an is with a view to the eventual 'ascension' of the believers from this world to the celestial abodes, which is what the process of salvation (*najah*) involves. For the contemplatives of Islam, the Ascension of the Prophet was the prototype of the mystic's own spiritual ascension to *Allah* via that ray of the Spirit connecting his soul to the Divinity.
>
> (Victor Danner, *The Islamic Tradition*, 48)

The Emigration (Hijrah)

The year 620 was marked by a double personal tragedy for Muhammad, with the death of his wife, Khadijah, and his uncle, Abu Talib. Khadijah had been the first to accept his Prophethood, and she had been his constant support and confidante, someone with whom he could share his concerns. Abu Talib had raised him from a small boy and, in the more troubled times of recent years, had protected him from the hostility of his tribe. Deprived of their protection and support, Muhammad found himself increasingly threatened by the powerful Quraysh.

Some 400 or so kilometres to the north of Mecca lay the oasis town of Yathrib. The town was inhabited by several tribes – two of which were Arabs, the rest Jewish – who were constantly warring with each other. A number of people from Yathrib had come into contact with Muhammad and his teachings and, during the pilgrimage to the Ka'ba in 621, they met him on a mountain pass outside Mecca. Over the next few months, more Yathibrites adopted the teachings of the Prophet. In 622, at the 'second treaty of the pass', Muhammad and his Meccan followers were invited to migrate to Yathrib, where they would be given protection. Shortly afterwards the Meccan Muslims began to slip away to Yathrib.

By September, the only Muslims remaining in Mecca were Muhammad and his closest companions. They, too, were ready to leave. The Quraysh were determined to stop them. To evade his persecutors Muhammad left Mecca and headed south, in the opposite direction to Yathrib, accompanied by Abu Bakr, one of his oldest and closest followers. The two men hid for three days in a cave on Mount Thawr, an hour's journey to the south of Mecca, until the hue and cry caused by their escape had abated. They then headed north to Yathrib, where in the months following Muhammad's arrival the first Islamic community (*umma*) was formed. In time the town came to be known by another name: *madinat al-nabi*, or Medina, the City of the Prophet.

The year (622) in which the emigration (*hijrah*) to Medina took place became the starting point of the Muslim lunar calendar – *Anno Hijarae* (AH). It is an appropriate point at which to interrupt the flow of historical events and open the Qur'an.

Chapter Two:

The Qur'an

The Opening (*Al-Fatihah*)

Bismi Llah ir-Rahman ir-Rahim

Il-hamdu li-Lahi rabb il-'alamin
Ar-rahman ir-Rahim
Maliki yawm id-din
Iyyaka na'budu wa iyyaka nasta'in
Ihdinas-sirat al-mustaqim
Sirat alladhina an'amta 'alayhim
Ghayril-maghdubi 'alayhim wa lad-dalin.

In the Name of Allah, the Beneficent, the Merciful.

Praise belongs to Allah, Lord of the Universe,
The Beneficent, the Merciful,
Master of the Day of Judgement.
Thee only do we serve; Thee alone do we ask for help.
Guide us in the Straight Path,
The path of those whom Thou hast blessed,
Not the path of those who incur Thy wrath,
Nor of those who have gone astray.

27

The first chapter (*surah*) of the Qur'an is named *Al-Fatihah* (literally, 'the Opening'). Also known as the 'Oft-Repeated Seven' (a reference to its seven verses), it is recited five times a day as part of the obligatory prayers (*salat*) and on many other occasions in the course of everyday public and private life.

The opening verse of the Qur'an which precedes the Fatihah – *Bismi Llah ir-Rahman ir-Rahim* ('In the Name of Allah, the Beneficent, the Merciful') – is repeated before each of the 114 surahs, except for Surah 9. Known as the *basmalah*, this particular consecrational formula is repeated before carrying out many daily duties or functions, such as eating or drinking, which might otherwise be performed mechanically, without conscious application or awareness.

The *basmalah* also expresses our fundamental relationship with the Divine Unity, for in its formula the Name of the absolute Oneness, *Allah*, is followed by two more Divine Names – *ar-Rahman* and *ar-Rahim* – both of which are derived from the same root, meaning 'Mercy'. The meanings given for *ar-Rahman* and *ar-Rahim* in traditional lists of the Ninety-Nine Divine Names are interchangeable, but between them they can be said to represent the creative flow and flux of the absolute Oneness. *Ar-Rahman* (the Beneficent, the Compassionate, also the Infinitely Good) conveys the outflow or outpouring of beneficence, the 'Outbreathing of the Compassionate'. Conversely, *ar-Rahim* (the Merciful) denotes the all-embracing Mercy, the 'Inbreathing', which draws us back to the Source from whence we come. This same sense of simultaneous flow and ebb, of a single cyclical pulse-like movement, is expressed in another much recited verse of the Qur'an: 'Verily we belong to Allah and verily unto Him we are returning.' (2:156) (For more on the Divine Names, also known as The Ninety-Nine Names, or The Most Beautiful Names, see Appendix: The Most Beautiful Names.)

Like the other Divine Names, *ar-Rahman* and *ar-Rahim* are described as 'attributes' of Allah and yet talking about them in the way we have just done might have given the impression that they are two separate activities or entities. That is one of the risks we run whenever we talk *about* the Divine Unity, for in doing so we take up a position as observer or commentator and attempt the impossible feat of placing ourselves outside that which, in reality, has no 'outside'. In thus distancing ourselves mentally from the One, we create a duality in our mind which, once established, is difficult to reconcile with what is imprinted on the innermost depths of our soul. As a consequence, at an existential level we experience a sense of separation from reality; or, to put it another way, we experience our individuality from the perspective of an existence that is somehow independent of the Divine Unity. We then try to overcome this profound existential contradiction by explaining it away in terms of the relationship between 'us' and 'God', thus perpetuating the dualism that is the origin of our dilemma. The Sufis are of one mind on this matter. 'I have put duality away. I have seen that the two worlds are one,' says Jalaluddin Rumi (d.1273). 'Take one step out of thyself, that thou mayst arrive at God,' counsels Abu Sa'id (d.1061). Al-Hallaj, who died a martyr's death in 922, is characteristically uncompromising: 'Whoso testifyeth that God is One thereby setteth up another beside Him (namely his own individual self as testifier).' As explained in Chapter 1, to attribute to ourselves (or to any being or thing) an existence that is outside or independent of the Divine Unity (*tawhid*) is to indulge in polytheism or associationism (*shirk*).

If we now return to the Fatihah we can see that it has three thematic parts. In the first three lines, we express our indebtedness and gratitude to Allah and His attributes *ar-Rahman* and *ar-Rahim*. In the fourth line, we acknowledge that we are here to serve the Divine Unity, upon which we are totally dependent for help and succour. In the remaining lines, we not only ask to be guided in the 'Straight Path' but we also ask not to err from the Path wantonly (thereby, metaphorically speaking, incurring the Divine Wrath) nor be led astray by our ignorance of it. In this way, the Fatihah expresses the essence of the Qur'an, an essence which is expressed even more succinctly in Surah 3: 'Surely, the [true] religion with Allah is Islam' (Qur'an 3:19). As we saw earlier, the word *islam* means the surrender of our whole being to the Will and Guidance of Allah.

The Formation of the Qur'an

The text of the Qur'an is divided into 114 surahs, varying in length from 3 to 286 verses and numbered according to the traditional order established within years of the death of the Prophet Muhammad. Each surah also has a title. In many cases, the title indicates the subject matter of the surah: Surah 12 'Yusuf' ('Joseph') is thus named because its subject is the life-story of Joseph, son of the biblical Jacob. Others take their title from a word or phrase within the surah: Surah 24 '*Al-Nur*' ('The Light'), takes its name from verses 35–40, which describe the Light of God and begin with the words: 'Allah is the Light of the heavens and the earth.' Yet others, such as Surah 20 '*Ta Ha*', take their title from the Arabic letters which form the first verse of the surah.

Joseph, the son of Jacob, is not the only biblical character to appear in the Qur'an. In calling for a return to the original religion of Abraham – that is, total surrender to the Divine Will – the Qur'an merely confirms what had previously been taught by Judaism and Christianity, the other Abrahamic religions, both of which had their own revealed teachings: the Torah of Moses and the Gospel of Jesus. In confirming this basic message, the Qur'an expounds afresh many of the traditional narratives and teachings contained in the Judaeo-Christian Bible: 'It (the Qur'an) confirms what was revealed before it and fully explains the Scriptures.' (Qur'an 10:37) Elsewhere in the same Surah (which is titled 'Noah'), we are told that there is no fundamental change in the message previously revealed to the Jews and Christians: 'There is no changing the Words of Allah.' (10:64) Indeed, the message at the heart of the Qur'an addressed itself to the Jews and Christians of Mecca and Medina as much as to the pagans – so as well as Abraham, Joseph and Noah, we find Adam, Moses and all the Prophets. We also find Jesus and his mother Mary.

The Qur'an concerns itself with far more than the pre-Islamic faiths. It relates certain events from the life of the Prophet, such as the Night Journey and Ascension, and tells of the battles fought between the Quraysh of Mecca and the Muslims of Medina; it lays down the basis of Islamic law and provides essential guidance on the conduct required of Muslims in both their secular and spiritual lives; and, above all else, it is the revealed Word of God, as shown in the words 'This Book is not to be doubted. It is a guide for the righteous, who have faith in the unseen . . .' (Qur'an 2:2–3)

Although the Fatihah is the first Surah of the Qur'an, it was not the first to be revealed. As we have already seen, the revelation of the Qur'an occurred progressively over a period of twenty-three years, beginning in Mecca and continuing in Medina. However, the arrangement of the surahs does not chronologically follow the order in which they were revealed. When each revelation occurred, the Prophet would indicate to his companions, or to his scribes, where it should be placed. Newly-revealed verses could be inserted into surahs that had already been revealed. In this way, verses revealed in Medina could be additions to a surah revealed in Mecca.

The surahs revealed in Mecca are generally shorter and more mystical, whereas those revealed in Medina are longer and more prosaic for they deal with aspects of religious and social law. These characteristic differences reflect the evolving nature of the early Islamic community. In Mecca, the original Companions of the Prophet were bound together by the intensity of their faith and their submission to the Will of Allah, whereas the expanded community at Medina was in need of guidance in the form of commands and prohibitions. As Professor Danner points out, the Meccan surahs are 'other-worldly'; the Medinan 'this-worldly'. More precisely, the Meccan surahs express the inner (esoteric) spiritual Path (*tariqah*), while the Medinan surahs express the outer (exoteric) Law (*shari'ah*). (Victor Danner, *The Islamic Tradition*, 47) Contrary to the order in which they were revealed, the very early Meccan surahs are placed at the end of the Qur'an while the lengthier, more exoteric and legalistic Medinan surahs are placed at the beginning. Commenting on this arrangement, the translator Marmaduke Pickthall explains: 'The inspiration of the Prophet progressed from inmost things to outward things, whereas most people find their way through outward things to things within.' (Marmaduke Pickthall, *The Meaning of the Glorious Koran*, 19)

The subtlety of the arrangement whereby the surahs lead us from the outer to the inner world echoes our own spiritual evolution as we travel along the Path that connects the two. Frithjof Schuon, author of many books on Islam and Sufism, describes the subtle workings of the Qur'an from a slightly different perspective:

> The Quran is, like the world, at the same time one and multiple. The world is a multiplicity which disperses and divides; the Quran is a multiplicity which draws together and leads to Unity. The multiplicity of the holy Book – the diversity of its words, sentences, pictures and stories – fills the soul and then absorbs it and imperceptibly transposes it into the climate of serenity and immutability by a sort of divine 'cunning'. The soul, which is accustomed to the flux of phenomena, yields to this flux without resistance; it lives in phenomena and is by them divided and

dispersed – even more than that, it actually becomes what it thinks
and does. The revealed Discourse has the virtue that it accepts this
tendency while at the same time reversing the movement thanks to
the celestial nature of the content and language, so that the fishes
of the soul swim without distrust and with their habitual rhythm
into the divine net.

(Frithjof Schuon, *Understanding Islam*, 48)

Various traditions describe how the Prophet was 'weighed down' by an
interior heaviness during the process of revelation. On one occasion, when
the revelation was delivered while he was seated upon a camel, his body
became so heavy that the camel found difficulty in supporting his weight. By
the time the revelation came to an end, the camel's legs were splayed out and
its under-belly was pressed against the ground. As new verses were revealed,
the Prophet would recite them aloud and his close followers (who are
frequently referred to as the 'Companions of the Prophet') would commit
them to memory. The verses were also written on a variety of materials –
including palm leaves, papyrus, leather, and animal bones – but the
transmission of the Qur'an was essentially an oral rather than written
tradition. At the time of the Prophet's death, tens of thousands of Muslims had
committed the Qur'an to memory, and its verses 'had a sacred presence in
their souls'. (Victor Danner, *The Islamic Tradition*, 64)

During the two-year reign of the Caliph Abu Bakr (d. 634), the Prophet's
immediate successor as head of the Islamic community, many of the early
Muslims who had memorized the Qur'an were killed in battle. Fearing that the
integrity of the Qur'an could be compromised, Abu Bakr ordered its collection
and a written copy to be made. Within thirty years, however, variations had
begun to appear in the recitation of the Qur'an and it was decided to agree a
definitive 'canonical' version, which was checked against the copy made by
Abu Bakr and the versions memorized by other Companions of the Prophet.
This definitive version was drawn up during the reign of the Caliph Uthman
(d. 656) and copies were sent to the principal Islamic cities of Basra,
Damascus, Kufa and Medina. (Two of these copies are still in existence: one is
in Tashkent, Uzbekistan; the other is in the Topkapi Palace in Istanbul.) The
text has since remained unaltered and so to recite the Qur'an in Arabic today

is to recite the Divine Word as it was revealed to Muhammad almost 1,400 years ago.

In one sense it is impossible to translate the Qur'an into a language other than Arabic, because a translation is not *the* Qur'an. Moreover, it is difficult to convey the rhythm of the language, the subtle nuances of meaning and the precise sense of the original. For this reason, translations of the Qur'an are sometimes referred to as 'interpretations' rather than 'translations' and, for the same reason, many non-Arabic books about Islam and/or the Sufis include a transliteration of the original Arabic word(s) alongside their rendering into English or other foreign languages. The Arabic word remains constant even though the words used to denote its meaning in a foreign language may vary from one author to the next.

Because the Qur'an was revealed in Arabic, Arabic remains the language in which it is recited, regardless of the nationality or mother tongue of those reciting it. Martin Lings notes that some Sufis who know very little Arabic nevertheless engage in a continuous reading of the Qur'an. If one objects that such an activity is of meagre benefit to the souls of those who have scant knowledge of the language they are reading, it could be answered that 'their minds are penetrated by the consciousness that they are partaking of the Divine Word. Their reading thus becomes the equivalent of a long drawn-out invocation of the Name *Allah*.' (Martin Lings, *What is Sufism?*, 25–6)

The Sufis and the Qur'an

In one of the discourses in his *Fihi ma fihi*, the Sufi Jalaluddin Rumi (d.1273) discusses the different ways in which people interpret the verse from the Qur'an in which Allah says: 'And We made the House to be a place of visitation for the people, and a sanctuary, saying: "Make of the place where Abraham stood to pray your place of prayer".' (2:125) According to Rumi, literalists interpret the 'House' in this verse to mean the Ka'ba in Mecca: since it is forbidden to do harm to any one there, it provides a sanctuary for all who take refuge. He adds that this understanding is 'all perfectly true and excellent' but it 'is the literal interpretation of the Qur'an'. The Qur'an can also be interpreted spiritually.

The Qur'an is a two-sided brocade. Some people enjoy one side, and some the other. Both are true, since God most High wishes that both groups of people might derive benefit from it. In the same way, a woman has a husband and a baby, each of whom enjoys her in a different way. The child's pleasure comes from her breast and her milk, that of the husband from intercourse and sharing a bed. Some people on the Path are like children drinking milk – they enjoy the literal meaning of the Qur'an. But those who are mature know of another kind of enjoyment and have a different understanding of the inner meanings of the Qur'an. (Jalaluddin Rumi, *Fihi ma fihi*. Discourse 44)

Rumi continues, saying that those who interpret the 'House' spiritually – that is, the Sufis – say that it refers to our inner world, which we ask God to cleanse of worldly desires and temptations so that it provides a sanctuary where we can commune with Him in peace and security.

For literalists, the 'place where Abraham stood to pray' is a particular spot near the Ka'ba where two cycles of prayer must be said. (The postures adopted while performing a cycle of prayer include standing, bowing from the waist, kneeling, and bending forward from a kneeling position to press the forehead on the ground.) Again Rumi says this is an excellent interpretation but, according to the Sufis, 'the place where Abraham stood to pray' means abandoning everything and sacrificing oneself entirely for the sake of God. Rumi adds that the performance of two cycles of prayer is again excellent, but the cycles should be prayed in such a way that the standing postures are performed in this world, the bowing postures in the other.

A further example of the Sufis' approach to the Qur'an is to be found in the teaching traditionally given by Imam 'Ali, the cousin and son-in-law of the Prophet, in response to a question from some of the Companions of the Prophet. They asked him what the Prophet had meant when he said: 'I am the city of knowledge and 'Ali is its gate.' 'Ali replied that all the Divine knowledge within the books of the prophets is contained within the Qur'an, and that all that is in the Qur'an is contained in the meaning of the opening Surah, the Fatihah. That which is in the Fatihah is itself contained within the opening phrase *Bismillah ir-Rahman ir-Rahim*. The secret meaning of this phrase is hidden within its first letter, the letter 'B'. That which is within all and everything is in the diacritical point beneath the (Arabic) letter 'B' (ﺏ). He concluded by saying: 'I am that point.'

When the Companions heard this they asked how it could all fit into a tiny dot. 'Ali replied: 'Knowledge is but a point. It is the ignorant who increased it.' Writing about this many centuries later, in his book, *Inspirations*, Shaykh Badruddin of Simawna (d.1420?) explained further:

> When the pen touches the paper, before it moves and writes a book, it first produces a dot. That point is the beginning and the essence of all the letters and words within the book. It contains them all.
>
> A place is entered through a door. Once one has passed through the door, one is in that space. This is a secret. If the mind understood it, it could stop thinking further. This small inspired work is like that dot, and what it contains, the heavens could not contain.
>
> *Bismillah ir-Rahman ir-Rahim* is the origin.
>
> All existence, seen and unseen, originates from the three Divine Names within this essential verse: *Allah*; *Rahman*, the All-Beneficent; and *Rahim*, the All-Merciful.'
>
> (Shaykh Badruddin of Simawna, *Inspirations*, 74)

Writing of 'the dot' in the twentieth century, Shaykh Ahmad al-Alawi (d.1934) said: 'Everything is enveloped in the Unity of Knowledge, symbolized by the Point.'

In the context of the above quotations, the 'dot' or 'point' may be compared to the 'infinitely compact and singular state' which, according to Big Bang theory, preceded the creation of the universe. Ever since the Big Bang the universe has been expanding, so that the further we are distanced by time from the Big Bang the more universe there is. Likewise, the further we are distanced by ignorance from the Unity of Knowledge the more there is for us to know. To repeat the words of Imam 'Ali: 'Knowledge is but a point. It is the ignorant who increased it.' It is with a view to removing the veils of ignorance that the Sufis seek out the inner meaning of the Qur'an.

The following brief selection from the Qur'an consists of passages that have especial significance for the Sufis. The first, which is one of many calls in the Qur'an to remember Allah, is associated with the practice of *dhikr* by the Sufis (*see* Glossary).

Remember Me. I will remember you.
(Surah 2, *The Cow*. 152)

Verily we belong to Allah and verily unto Him we are returning.
(Surah 2, *The Cow*. 156)

And when My servants question thee concerning Me, tell them that I am very near. I answer the prayer of the suppliant when he calls Me. So let them answer My call and trust in Me, that they may be rightly guided.
(Surah 2, *The Cow*. 186)

It is not the eyes that are blind but the hearts.
(Surah 22, *Pilgrimage*. 46)

Allah is the Light of the heavens and the earth. His Light is like a niche wherein is a lamp. The lamp is encased in glass, the glass shines with star-like brilliance. It is lit from a blessed tree, an olive neither of the East nor of the West, whose oil would almost shine forth (of itself), even though no fire touched it. Light upon light. Allah guides to His light whom He will. And Allah speaks to mankind in allegories, for Allah is Knower of all things . . . The one from whom Allah withholds His light shall find no light at all. Have you not seen how all in the heavens and in the earth give praise to Allah, even the birds on the wing? He knows the prayer and praise of all His creatures, and Allah knows their actions. Allah's is the sovereignty of the heavens and the earth, and to Him all things return.

(Surah 24, *Light*. 35, 40–42)

We indeed created man; and We know the whisperings of his soul, and

We are nearer to him than his jugular vein.

(Surah 50, *Qaf*. 15)

And in the earth are signs for those of real faith, and in yourselves.
What! Can you not see?

(Surah 51, *The Winnowing Winds*. 20–21)

Everything upon the earth shall pass away; but the Face of thy Lord shall remain for ever, resplendent with Majesty and Glory.

(Surah 55, *The Beneficent*. 26–7)

> Say: Allah is One! Eternal.
> All things depend on Him.
> He begetteth not, and He is not begotten,
> And there is none like unto Him.
> (Surah 112, *The Unity*)

Chapter Three:

The Foundations of Islam

From Medina to the Caliphate
Medina and Jihad

The year of the *Hijrah* (622) had seen the emigration of the Prophet and his followers from Mecca to Medina. In that same year the Islamic community at Medina had come under attack by the Meccans, resulting in the launch of *Jihad*. The word *jihad*, usually translated as 'Holy War', is derived from a root verb meaning to 'strive', 'struggle', or 'exert'. In its outer (exoteric) sense, *jihad* refers to the defence of Islam and the Islamic community, whereas in its inner (esoteric) sense it refers to self-purification and the 'war' against the ego or lower self. The order of priority in these two types of *jihad* was the subject of a remark made by the Prophet to his companions as they returned home after a battle: 'We are returning from the lesser Holy War to the Greater Holy War.' They were returning from the conflict with their outward enemies to face the conflict within themselves.

The Sufis see the relationship between events in the outer and inner worlds as constant for, according to a *hadith* of the Prophet, 'Whoso knoweth himself knoweth his Lord'. Or again, as Ibn al-Farid (d.1235) said: 'I was sent from myself as a messenger to myself and my essence testified to myself by my signs.' That is, if we were able to understand our underlying motives for doing the things we do in the outer world, we would understand what is going on in our inner world –

and vice versa – for as Jalaluddin Rumi said: ' . . . the two worlds are one'. The historical events related here can be understood within this one-world context.

Early skirmishes with the Quraysh soon gave way to full-scale warfare, and by the end of the decade the Prophet had succeeded in uniting the Bedouin tribes of the Arabian Peninsula. In 630, he marched on Mecca with an army of 10,000. The city capitulated and the pagan idols in the Ka'ba were destroyed. Soon, thousands converted to Islam, yet the Prophet was aware that many had done so for the sake of expediency and a share in the spoils of war.

In 632, the Prophet made what is now known as the 'Pilgrimage of Farewell', the first full Islamic pilgrimage to Mecca, during which he established the traditional rituals that have been followed by Muslims ever since. Shortly after his return to Medina he was taken ill and he passed away in June of that year.

The Caliphate

Following the death of the Prophet there was a degree of confusion among his close followers, not only about who should succeed him as Caliph but also about how the choice should be made. ('Caliph' is the anglicized form of *khalifah*. In the Qur'an, man is called the *khalifah* – meaning 'representative' or 'vicegerent' – of God.) In the two years since the *Hijrah* the ranks of the Prophet's closest followers had swollen, and they now formed three clearly identifiable groups. The first of these, which included Abu Bakr, 'Umar, 'Uthman, and 'Ali, comprised the loyal companions who had been with him in Mecca and had migrated with him to Medina. A second group was made up of the prominent Medinans who had accepted the Prophet's teachings and, by inviting him to Medina, had enabled the first Islamic community to be established. The third group was formed by recent converts to Islam, many from the leading families of Mecca, including some who until recently had been the Prophet's enemies. It was members of this latter group who would eventually rise to power.

The immediate confusion over the succession arose because some of the Prophet's followers believed that before he died he had declared that 'Ali, his cousin and son-in-law, was to be his heir and successor. ('Ali was the son of Abu Talib, the Prophet's maternal uncle and guardian, and had married Fatimah, daughter of the Prophet and Khadijah.) In the event, however, a group of Medinan elders elected Abu Bakr, the Prophet's close companion and father-in-law, as the new leader. (The Prophet had remarried more than once after the death of Khadijah, his first wife, and tradition relates that of these later wives his favourite was 'A'isha, the daughter of Abu Bakr.)

With the death of the Prophet, old tribal rivalries and suspicions came to the surface and some dissenting tribes immediately rebelled against the leadership of Abu Bakr. He put down the rebellion, but these tribal wars continued throughout most of his short-lived caliphate (632–634). It was during his rule that Islam began to spread beyond the confines of Arabia, with the Islamic armies conquering parts of Syria and Persia. On his death in battle in 634, he was succeeded by 'Umar ibn al-Khattab, another Companion of the Prophet, under whom the expansion of Islam continued. Considerable territorial gains were made at the expense of the Byzantine Empire, with the conquest of Syria, Palestine, Egypt and parts of North Africa; and the powerful Sassanian Persian Empire was all but destroyed. The most significant gain, however, was the capture of Jerusalem, the Holy City of the three Abrahamic religions, for it was from here that the Prophet had ascended to the gates of heaven at the *Mi'raj*. It was during 'Umar's rule that most of the institutions of Islamic government – financial, military, and judicial – were established, and the year of the *Hijrah* was adopted as the starting point of the Islamic calendar.

'Umar was assassinated in 644 and his successor, 'Uthman ibn 'Afan, a member of the 'Ummayad clan of the Quraysh tribe, was nominated by a group of Medinan elders. Not only was his succession controversial but 'Uthman also fanned the flames of future unrest when he appointed numerous members of his own clan to key positions. Military success continued under his rule with the fall of the Persian city of Persepolis, the centre of the Zoroastrian religion. The Muslim conquests now reached out across the sea with the capture of Cyprus, Sicily, Rhodes and many Mediterranean ports. However, 'Uthman is considered to have used the semi-

sacred position of Caliph to further the interests of himself and his family –
accusations of nepotism and the misappropriation of state funds were levelled
against him. His strongest critics and opponents were a group formed by the
Prophet's relatives and companions, as well as many of the earliest converts to
Islam. After 'Uthman's murder in 656, 'Ali, the Prophet's cousin and son-in-law,
was elected as the Fourth Caliph.

Support for 'Ali was not unanimous. Open hostility was displayed by
Mu'awiyah, cousin of 'Uthman, governor of Syria, and leader of the Ummayad
clan. Civil war erupted, and the opposing armies of 'Ali and Mu'awiyah fought at
the battle of Siffin in 657. In the interests of unity, 'Ali sought a compromise with
his opponents, which provoked dissent among his own supporters, the Shi'i (or
shi'ah, from *shi'atu 'Ali*, 'the party of 'Ali'). A group of dissenters, later known as
the *Khariji* ('secessionists'; literally 'those who go out'), left 'Ali's camp. With the
assassination of 'Ali by a member of the *Khariji* in 661, the caliphate of those
who had been closest to the Prophet – the 'orthodox' or 'Rightly-Guided'
Caliphs, as the first four caliphs are known – effectively came to an end.

'Ali's appointed successor was his eldest son Hasan who, in order to avoid
further bloodshed, accepted a truce with Mu'awiyah. When the latter was
declared Caliph in 661, the seat of the caliphate moved to Damascus from
where he stamped out any dissent. Writing about this crucial period in the
evolution of Islam, Shaykh Fadhlalla Haeri says:

> Many pious Muslims regard this era as that of betrayal and
> subversion of the true original prophetic model.
>
> In the name of Islam an empire was created, taking as its
> capital the ancient Byzantine city of Damascus and adopting the
> administrative, political and military machinery of the defunct
> Byzantine government. From this point on most Muslim rulers and
> their governments grew more concerned with self-preservation,
> power, accumulating wealth and controlling their people. The
> prophetic way of piety and submission to Allah's decree,
> establishing justice and Islam, came to be upheld only at face value.
> (Shaykh Fadhlalla Haeri, *The Elements of Islam*, 80)

This period also witnessed the division of Muslims into Sunni and Shi'i, a division triggered largely by the issue of leadership. Whereas Sunni Muslims accept the line of elected Caliphs, the Shi'i (the 'party of 'Ali') hold that the rightful leader (*imam*) of the Islamic community was Imam 'Ali. They also hold that the Imamate should have been hereditary and that ever since the murder of Imam 'Ali the Caliphate has been in the hands of usurpers. As it was, Imam 'Ali's first son, Imam Hasan, is said to have been poisoned, while his second son, Imam Husayn, who attempted to regain the caliphate, was killed at the battle of Karbala on the banks of the Euphrates, on 10 October 680, by the army of the Caliph Yazid, son of the now deceased Mu'awiyah. Karbala, where Husayn is buried, has since become a holy city of the Shi'i and a place of pilgrimage. Imam Husayn's tomb, like that of his father, Imam 'Ali, at Kufah (modern Najaf), is one of the greatest shrines of the Shi'i. The day of Imam Husayn's death (10 Muharram on the Hijri calendar) is commemorated every year by the Shi'i in their most important religious festival, Ashura, which is a day of mourning and lamentation.

The Elements of Islam

The preceding brief overview of the period from the *Hijrah* to the death of Imam Husayn has, in more than one sense, brought us to a parting of the ways. The expansion of Islam into an empire which stretched from the Atlantic coasts of Spain and Portugal in the west to the borders of China in the east lies outside the scope of this book. So, too, does the immense artistic and scientific contribution Islamic civilization has made to the world's cultural heritage. These aspects, together with the (often subtle) influence that Islam has exercised on our own European cultural tradition, are dealt with in detail in numerous other books.

Within a Sufi context, however, the spread of Islam out into the world can perhaps be understood in the light of a traditional *hadith qudsi* ('Divine Tradition'): 'I was a hidden treasure and I longed to be known, so I created the world that I might be known.' To human eyes, the Divine Unity manifests as a multiplicity of physical phenomena on the material plane, each of which appears to have an existence of its own. This is a natural part of the 'stepping down' process by which spiritual reality manifests on the material or phenomenal plane and higher truths are translated into a form that can be more readily understood by the lower self. In spite of appearances, however, there is unity in multiplicity. As the original spiritual impulse of Islam and the teachings of the Prophet spread out into the world, it was inevitable that they would undergo a gradual process of dilution and corruption. The same had happened with the earlier Abrahamic religions of Judaism and Christianity.

To quote again the words of Imam 'Ali: 'Knowledge is but a point. It is the ignorant who increased it.' The world of phenomena – which many today refer to as the 'real world' – can either lead us towards knowledge of the Divine Unity or it can lead us away from it. This is one interpretation of the two paths referred to in the Fatihah: the Straight Path, and the path of those who have gone astray. For the Sufis there was (and is) only One Path and they emerged onto the historical stage, and exercised a corrective influence, at a time when the rapid territorial spread of Islam brought with it unprecedented riches and an imbalance between outer and inner realities. The first Sufis, therefore, emphasized the ascetic life. Later on, when the religion was in danger of becoming too exoteric and legalistic, the Sufi influence revivified its spiritual essence.

We shall be returning to the role of the Sufis in the next chapter. For the present, however, we will turn to those aspects of the Islamic religion which were established by the Prophet and which, in the outer law or *shari'ah*, provided the framework for a path leading to inner awakening and submission to the Divine Will.

The *Sunnah* of the Prophet

As we have seen, the Prophet succeeded in uniting the tribes of Arabia into a single Islamic nation. Although this unity began to unravel in a revival of tribal differences and loyalties in the period following his death, the religion of Islam provided an underlying unity that held the nation together. The religion also provided a stability in that the Prophet had not only set the practical example of what was required of Muslims in their outer and inner lives, he had also left them with clear instructions to follow. This combination of example and instruction is known as the *Sunnah* of the Prophet, or the Prophetic (or Muhammadan) Norm. As Professor Danner explains, this gives Islam a unique quality:

> Of all the major religions still extant, Islam is the only one that is essentially the same now as it was in the days of its founder. As a result, the Muslim, whether in the Middle Ages or now, has nothing to invent or devise for himself. The manuals on Islam simply describe the beliefs and practices of the Prophet, as embodied in his Sunnah. The Muslim seeking a pious life merely follows the patterns established by the Prophet; the fervour he brings to his religion is what enlivens those patterns and gives them their inner life.
>
> (Victor Danner, *The Islamic Tradition*, 50)

Professor Danner continues, contrasting the Sunnah of the Prophet with that of the Buddha, describing the latter as:

> . . . purely contemplative and meant almost exclusively for monks, even though some provisions were made for laymen during and after the Buddha's mission. This clearly was not the case for the Sunnah of the Prophet which contained a mystical or contemplative essence, as in Buddhism, as well as prescriptions for the life of action that applied to the *entire* community. There were no laymen in Islam.
>
> (Victor Danner, *The Islamic Tradition*, 50)

There were no monks, either. Sufis practise the principle of being *in* the world but not *of* the world. Abu Sa'id ibn Abi 'l Khayr (d.1049) expressed the principle thus: 'The true saint (or 'friend of God' as the Sufis are called) goes in and out amongst the people and eats and sleeps with them and buys and sells in the market and marries and takes part in social intercourse, and never forgets God for a single moment.' That is to say, the Sufi is *in* the world but not *attached* to the world, for he/she belongs to God. The principle of non-attachment to the world is expressed in a saying (*hadith*) of the Prophet: 'Be in this world as a stranger or as a passer-by'.

From its inception, Islam had a strong oral tradition. The memorization and transmission of the Qur'an by the Companions of the Prophet was accompanied by a similar memorization and transmission of the actions and sayings of the Prophet. Known as Prophetic Traditions, these actions and sayings were collected together after his death and recorded along with the lineage by which the tradition had been transmitted. The recorded statements or *ahadith* (singular, *hadith*), which form the basis of the Sunnah, fall into two kinds: those spoken by the Prophet on his own authority (*ahadith nabawi*) and those in which the Prophet serves as the mouthpiece of Allah (*ahadith qudsi*). With both kinds of *ahadith* the Sufis look for the inner meaning.

Iman, *Islam*, and *Ihsan*

A *hadith* reported by the Caliph 'Umar, one of the Companions of the Prophet, concerns three elements which together form the basis of the Islamic religion. They are *iman* (faith), *islam* (submission to the Divine Will) and *ihsan* (virtue, or the spiritual life).

> One day when we were with the Messenger of God there came unto us a man whose clothes were of exceeding whiteness and whose hair was of exceeding blackness, nor were there any signs of travel upon him, although none of us had seen him before. He sat down knee unto knee opposite the Prophet, upon whose thighs he placed the palms of his hands, saying: 'O Muhammad, tell me what is the surrender unto God (*al-islam*).' The Prophet answered: 'The surrender is that thou shouldst perform the prayer, bestow the alms, fast Ramadan, and make, if thou canst, the pilgrimage to the Holy House.' He said: 'Thou hast spoken truly' and we were amazed that having questioned him he should corroborate him.

> Then he said: 'Tell me what is faith (*iman*)', and the Prophet
> answered: 'It is that thou shouldst believe in God and His Angels
> and His Books and His Apostles and the Last Day, and thou
> shouldst believe that no good or evil cometh but by His
> Providence.' 'Thou hast spoken truly,' he said, and then: 'Tell me
> what is excellence (*ihsan*).' The Prophet answered: 'It is that thou
> shouldst worship God as if thou sawest Him, for if thou seest Him
> not, verily He seeth thee' . . . Then the stranger went away, and I
> stayed there long after he had gone, until the Prophet said to me:
> 'O 'Umar, knowest thou the questioner, who he was?' I said: 'God
> and His Prophet know best, but I know not at all.' 'It was Gabriel'
> said the Prophet. 'He came to teach you your religion.'
> (Translated by Martin Lings, *A Sufi Saint of the Twentieth Century*, 44)

The Sufis frequently refer to other *ahadith*, or to passages from the Qur'an,
which they see as relating to these three fundamental elements of Islam. For
example, the integrated approach to *iman* practised by the Sufis is the subject
of an often-quoted *hadith*: 'Faith (*iman*) is a knowledge in the heart, a voicing
with the tongue, and an activity with the limbs.' The definition of *ihsan*
contained in the *hadith* reported by 'Umar is often quoted in Sufi material. An
alternative rendering is: 'Worship God as if you saw Him, for if you do not see
Him (inwardly, with the eye of the heart), He sees you.' The following *hadith
qudsi*, much quoted by the Sufis, expresses the essence of *islam* succinctly:
'Die before you die'.

The *hadith* reported by Caliph 'Umar also outlines what have become
known as the 'Five Pillars of Islam', the sacred practices to be performed by
Muslims – comprising prayer, almsgiving, the fast of Ramadan and (if possible)
the pilgrimage to the Ka'ba in Mecca. The fifth pillar is the *shahadah*, or
declaration of faith, from which everything else derives. An important aspect
of the Five Pillars is the intention with which they are performed: to execute
them mechanically or without the prescribed preparatory purification renders
them invalid. Sufis and others have defined three levels of intention –
motivation might be a better word – beginning in the outer world, with the

motivation provided by the obligation to fulfil the religious law (*shari'ah*), and leading progressively towards being motivated by the inner truth (*haqiqah*).

Shari'ah, *Tariqah* and *Haqiqah*

The Sufi understanding of the relationship between the inner and outer worlds has already been mentioned. Like most things pertaining to Islam, the relationship between the two is the subject of a *hadith*:

> The outer law *(shari'ah)* is my word,
> the spiritual path (*tariqah*) my actions,
> and the inner reality (*haqiqah*) my inner states.

In recent years the Western media have reported many instances of the application of *shari'ah* law that have appalled Western sensitivities: public stoning to death for adultery, public lashings for various offences, amputation of hands for theft and so on. The application of *shari'ah* in these instances is not to be confused with the *shari'ah* of the Sufis, even though they are one and the same. These things are a matter of interpretation. Is the *shari'ah* intended to be interpreted to the letter – that is, literally – or spiritually? In answering this question the Sufis say:

> Whoever has the outer law without the inner reality
> has left the right way;
> Whoever has the inner reality without the outer law
> is a heretic.
> Whoever unites the two of them has realization.

Shari'ah concerns itself with the way in which we conduct ourselves in the phenomenal world. It provides the outer framework within which both the individual and society may evolve towards inner awakening and higher consciousness. *Haqiqah* is from the same root as *al-haqq*, meaning 'truth'. It refers to an immutable inner reality. These two realities – the outer and inner

– can be equated with the way in which we both perceive and experience life. They are also related to our organs of sense perception: *shari'ah* to the gross physical senses, *haqiqah* to the subtle spiritual senses. If we approach *shari'ah* from the viewpoint of *haqiqah*, its inner meaning and spirit are immediately obvious. On the other hand, if we approach *shari'ah* from its own viewpoint, we remain in ignorance of its inner meaning. What we have is a literal interpretation of the outer reality. A similar principle applies to *haqiqah*, hence the need for the spiritual path or method (*tariqah*), for it binds together the otherwise dualistic realities of the inner and outer worlds.

The three mind-sets, or approaches to the spiritual path, associated with *shari'ah*, *tariqah* and *haqiqah* are described more fully in *Inner Secrets of the Path*, written by Sayyid Haydar Amuli in the fourteenth century. Sayyid Amuli defines three categories of Muslim, whom he associates with the three Abrahamic revelations. The first comprises the scholars and those trained in jurisprudence – the jurists (*fuqaha'*) or religious lawyers – whom he likens to Moses in their perfection of the outer dimension. Within the second category are the philosophers, whom he likens to Jesus in their perfection of the inner dimension. In the third category, he places the gnostics and other enlightened people, likening them to Muhammad in their perfection of both the inner and outer dimensions and the way in which they live their lives according to the three principles of *shari'ah* (outer law), *tariqah* (spiritual path) and *haqiqah* (inner reality).

Sayyid Amuli illustrates this last point with a metaphor in which he likens the *shari'ah* to a river and *haqiqah* to an ocean. He says that the jurists keep to the banks of the river and the philosophers dive for pearls in the ocean, while the gnostics ride in boats to safety. These three categories can also be applied to people in general, and he names them respectively as the people of *shari'ah*, the people of *tariqah* and the people of *haqiqah*. (Sayyid Amuli, Inner Secrets of the Path, 39)

We can perhaps further describe the subjects of Sayyid Amuli's categories as the literalists, the travellers and those who have arrived. As such, they recall Marmaduke Pickthall's comment on the arrangement of the Qur'an: 'The inspiration of the Prophet progressed from inmost things to outward things,

whereas most people find their way through outward things to things within.'
A similar inspiration lies behind the establishment of the Five Pillars of Islam
and gives them their inner meaning.

The Five Pillars of Islam

> And (as for) true believers, both men and women, they are friendly
> guardians of each other; they enjoin what is right and forbid what
> is evil; they attend to their prayers and pay the alms-tax, and obey
> Allah and His messenger. On these Allah will show mercy. Surely
> Allah is Mighty, Wise.
> (Qur'an 9:71)

*The Creed (*Shahadah*)*

The foundation stone of Islam is the formula known as the *shahadah* (the
Creed, or Testimony of Faith), which states: *La ilaha illa 'Llah,
Muhammadun rasulu 'Llah* ('There is no divinity except Allah, Muhammad is
the Messenger of Allah'). The subtleties of the formula have been written
about at length, notably the negation and affirmation contained in the first
part of the statement: 'There is no divinity' (negation) 'except Allah'
(affirmation). The formula is such that it can be used with any one of the Most
Beautiful Names (the Attributes or Qualities of Allah). Victor Danner cites the
example of the Guide (*al-Hadi*): 'When one says . . . "There is no guide except
the Guide", one is denying that anyone but God could guide, for God alone is
the Guide. Or one is affirming that whatever guidance a creature has is really
that of the Divine Guide.' (Victor Danner, *The Islamic Tradition*, 5) Further
examples are: 'There is no truth except the Truth', 'There is no self-existing
one except the Self-Existing One', 'There is no friend except the Friend', and
so on.

The second part of the *shahadah* states: 'Muhammad is the Messenger of
God'. Muhammad is both 'Prophet' and 'Messenger', a Messenger being the
founder of a religion whereas a Prophet is one who renews the Message

delivered previously by a Messenger. There had been many Prophets before Muhammad in the Abrahamic dispensation, but he is known as the 'Seal of the Prophets' (the last Prophet) because his teaching represents the completion of the teachings. By contrast, there were few Messengers. From the Islamic viewpoint Abraham, Moses, and Jesus are all Prophets and Messengers. They also practised *islam* since they each surrendered to the Divine Will with their whole being.

*Prayer (*Salat*)*

The obligatory prayers are performed five times a day, at certain prescribed times – dawn, noon, mid-afternoon, sunset and night-time. On Friday, the day of gathering, Muslims collect in the main mosque of a town to say noon prayers together. *Salat* is preceded by a simple ablution or ritual washing (*wudu*), which consists of washing the hands, rinsing the mouth and nostrils, wiping the entire face, washing the forearms from wrists to elbows, wiping over the head and the back of the neck and washing the feet. Outwardly, *wudu* is a cleansing of physical dirt from the body, but the washing of the limbs also symbolizes a purification of one's outward actions and the intention behind them. It is a time for cleansing the mind, too, by driving out trivial and/or negative thoughts in preparation for prayer. The place of prayer must also be clean.

Salat itself is performed when facing in the direction of the Ka'ba in Mecca, the symbolic House of God originally built by Abraham. Certain prayers and passages from the Qur'an, including the Fatihah, are recited in a precise order while adopting three specific postures: standing (*qiyam*), bowing (*ruku*) and prostration (*sajdah*). Shaykh Fadhlalla Haeri describes the inner significance of the three postures thus, beginning with the initial standing posture:

> While one stands in wonderment and adoration, one is calling upon the mercy of God. When one realizes the immensity of divine power one is so awe-struck that one bows in the face of such majesty. And finally one disappears from existence – all that is other

than Allah – by prostrating oneself. In prostration one's individual profile and locus of sensory experience (the face) is obliterated in the dust of the earth. As all sensual awareness recedes, inner awareness is enhanced.

(Shaykh Fadhlalla Haeri, *The Elements of Islam*, 38)

In his *Book of Sufi Healing*, Shaykh Moinuddin Chishti remarks that the performance of *salat* at the prescribed times of day attunes one to the movements of the planets and variations of the seasons in such a way that one is in harmony with the natural cycles of the universe. He also outlines the beneficial effects – physical, psychological, and spiritual – of the postures adopted for the obligatory prayers, and of the sound vibrations created by the recitation of the prayers in Arabic. He notes that each cycle of prayer (*ra'kah*) comprises seven different postures, and that a minimum of seventeen *ra'kahs* are performed in the course of a day, making a total of 119 postures each day. Simply as a physical activity, *salat* is something that people of all ages can do. It is also said to assist physical development. (Shaykh Moinuddin Chishti, *The Book of Sufi Healing*, 93, 103)

Alms-giving (Zakat)

Zakat is the obligatory annual giving to the poor by adult Muslims. Originally it was a tax levied on material goods once they exceeded a certain threshold. In today's world, where most people's wealth is measured in monetary terms, Muslims give about two and a half per cent of their income.

The root from which the word *zakat* is derived means 'to purify' and 'to increase', so the obligation to give alms also has an inner, purifying function. It not only 'purifies' the donor's wealth, it also encourages a charitable, generous disposition, and a non-attachment to worldly possessions. Moreover, it acknowledges that we all have a duty of care towards our fellow beings within the Divine Unity, especially those who are less well off than ourselves.

For Sayyid Amuli, the emphasis of *zakat* is on purification. The 'people of *tariqah*' give the *zakat* as prescribed by the *shari'ah* and they are then obliged to purify the soul of miserliness and cleanse the heart of meanness. One of the secrets of *zakat*, says Amuli, is that it has the power to do these things. The *zakat* of the people of *haqiqah* 'refers to the removal of the awareness of limitation from everything in existence and causing each to arrive at the world of the unrestricted or absolute, such that it becomes purified of the stain of otherness and the impurity of duality'. (Sayyid Amuli, *Inner Secrets of the Path*, 261, 267)

*Fasting (*Sawm*)*

Ramadan, the ninth month of the Muslim calendar, is the month of obligatory fasting during which one abstains from all intake of food and drink, as well as smoking and sexual activity, between dawn and sunset. A pre-fast meal is usually taken before dawn, and the meal that breaks the fast after sunset can be a celebratory social occasion. Because the Islamic calendar is lunar rather than solar, the year is 354 days long, which means that the months shift backwards eleven days every year, so it takes just over thirty-one solar years to complete a full cycle. Consequently, the month-long fast of Ramadan can occur at different seasons of the year. In equatorial countries, the hours of daylight and darkness remain relatively balanced, but in countries beyond the tropics the hours of daylight can be considerably longer in summer, making the hours of fasting correspondingly longer too. According to tradition, the night the Qur'an 'came down' – the Night of Power – occurred in Ramadan. The month of fasting builds up to the Night of Power, which generally falls on 27 Ramadan but is dependent on the timing of the new moon.

The extent of the potential benefits of the fast depends largely on the intention of those fasting. According to Sayyid Amuli, the people of *tariqah* perform the prescribed fast (as practised by the people of *shari'ah*) but also refrain from things that might stimulate the outer senses of sight, sound, smell, touch and taste. For example: violent images; raucous sounds, gossip, or slander; obnoxious or sweet smells; touching things beyond moderation, or to excess; eating and drinking to excess; and consuming that which has been taken from the poor or acquired by usury.

The inner senses are included in the fast in that one abstains from using them for anything other than that for which they were created. For example, concerning the faculty of memory, Sayyid Amuli says: 'Since the faculty of thought has only been created to reflect upon divine gnosis and intellectual knowledge and the like, things other than these should not exist in its storehouse.' He makes a similar comment about the faculty of imagination, observing that it should be used solely for seeing the meaning of events clearly; we should not allow it to transport us into the realms of fantasy or fear. The people of *haqiqah* perform the two kinds of fast practised by the people of *shari'ah* and *tariqah*. In addition they abstain 'from witnessing anything other than the Real whatever the circumstances – in accordance with the judgement of the men of this science: "There is nothing in existence but Allah, His Names, Attributes and Actions; all is He, by Him, from Him and to Him". ' (Sayyid Amuli, *Inner Secrets of the Path*, 243–256)

*Pilgrimage (*Hajj*)*

In Chapter 1 we saw how the sanctuary or sacred precinct at Mecca had been a place of pilgrimage for Arabs for centuries and that part of their pilgrimage entailed circumambulating the Ka'ba. The Prophet destroyed the pagan idols in the Ka'ba when he took the city of Mecca in 630, and he performed the first full Islamic *Hajj* in 632, the year he died. It is incumbent upon Muslims, but not obligatory, to undertake the pilgrimage to Mecca at least once in their lifetime. The minor pilgrimage (*'Umrah*) may be performed at any time of the year, but the full annual pilgrimage takes place during the month of *Dhu 'l-hijja*, the twelfth month of the lunar calendar. The various elements, which are performed over a number of days, commemorate events in the lives of Abraham, Ishmael and Hagar when they were in the region of Mecca. They are described here in a fair amount of detail because, as we will see, they also have a corresponding inner dimension.

As the pilgrims approach Mecca they stop at one of several designated places at a certain distance from the city, in order to put on the special pilgrim's costume (*ihram*) which consists of two unsewn pieces of white cloth, one of which is tucked around the waist while the other is draped around the shoulders. In the process the pilgrim divests him/herself of all outward signs of status and individuality and enters a state of consecration (also denoted by the word *ihram*) for the duration of the pilgrimage.

The first major element of the *hajj* is the circumambulation of the Ka'ba (*tawaf*) – seven times in an anti-clockwise direction. Although not an obligatory part of the *hajj*, the pilgrim may next drink from the Well of Zamzam, the spring of water that Allah caused to emerge from the ground when Hagar and Ishmael were dying of thirst in the desert. (The spring, which flows beneath the Great Mosque, takes its name from the Arabic word *zam*, meaning 'stop', because the water gushed out of the ground so fast that Hagar shouted: '*zam! zam!* – 'stop! stop!'.)

The second obligatory act is the *sa'i* ('hastening'), which entails passing seven times between the two hills of Safa and Marwa (symbolizing caution and hope) at a fast walk or run, in emulation of Hagar's increasingly frantic search for water in the desert. The performance of *sa'i* is said to symbolize our striving for personal gain in the world, in the course of which we run hither and thither at an ever faster pace in search of that which eludes us.

Next comes the standing in prayer from noon until sunset on the plain beneath the slopes of Mount Arafat. (The word *arafat* is derived from a root meaning 'common knowledge'.) It is estimated that between two and three million pilgrims, all wearing the white *ihram*, gather here in one assembly to pray, after which they travel to Mina. On the way they stop overnight at Muzdalifah, a barren place in the desert, where the sunset and night prayers are said. While they are there they also collect a number of pebbles which will be used for stoning the three stone pillars at Mina. The pillars represent Satan and the stoning of them re-enacts Abraham's temptation not to submit to the Divine Will and sacrifice his offspring. At an inner level the stoning symbolizes the rejection of the temptation to be distracted from the Path by our this-worldly desires.

The climax of the *Hajj* occurs on the tenth day of the month with the Feast of Sacrifice (*'id al-adha*), celebrated simultaneously throughout the Islamic world to commemorate the animal sacrifice Abraham made in place of his son.

Whereas the stoning of the pillars symbolizes the rejection of all that comes between us and the Divine, the animal sacrifice represents the surrender to the Divine Will which is concomitant with the sacrifice of the lower (or animal) self.

The following anecdotal story about a *hajji* (a person who has made the pilgrimage to Mecca) makes the point that outer ritual alone serves little or no spiritual purpose unless it is performed with a conscious inner intent. The story also involves Imam Junayd of Baghdad (d.910), who is considered by many Sufis to have been one of the greatest among them.

Imam Junayd was approached by a man who had just returned from the *hajj*. Junayd asked him: 'From the moment you first set off from home on your travels have you also been travelling away from your sins?'

'No,' replied the man.

'Then you have not travelled,' said Junayd. 'At each stage of your journey, when you stopped for the night did you negotiate a stage on the Path to God?'

'No.'

'Then you have not trodden the Path, stage by stage,' said Junayd. 'When you put on the garment worn by pilgrims at the designated place, as you took off your clothes did you discard the qualities of your human nature?'

'No.'

'Then you have not put on the pilgrim's garment. When you stood at Arafat, did you stand a moment in contemplation of God?'

'No.'

'Then you have not stood at Arafat. When you went to Muzdalifa and achieved your desire, did you renounce all sensual desires?'

'No.'

'Then you have not gone to Muzdalifa. When you circumambulated the Ka'ba, did you behold the spiritual beauty of God in the abode of purification?'

'No.'

'Then you have not circumambulated the Ka'ba. When you hastened between Safa and Marwa, did you attain to purity (*safa*) and virtue (*muruwwat*)?'

'No.'

'Then you have not hastened. When you were at Mina, did all your wishes (*muna*) cease?

'No.'

'Then you have not yet visited Mina. When you reached the place of slaughter and offered sacrifice, did you sacrifice the objects of worldly desire?'

'No.'

'Then you have not sacrificed. When you threw the pebbles, did you throw away whatever sensual thoughts were accompanying you?'

'No.'

'Then you have not yet thrown the pebbles, and you have not yet performed the *hajj*.'

Chapter Four:

The Sufis

The name 'Sufi'

Jalaluddin Rumi tells a story about an elephant that was put on exhibition. A large crowd of people gathered to see it, undeterred by the fact that the elephant was displayed in a darkened room. Because there was not enough light to see the elephant by, they felt it in the dark with their hands. One person felt its trunk and declared that the animal was like a water-pipe. Another felt its ear, and said it was like a large fan. A third, who felt its leg, said it was like a pillar. Yet another, who felt the elephant's back, claimed it was like a large throne. Depending on which part of the elephant they touched, each person gave a different description of the animal. (Jalaluddin Rumi, *Mathnawi*, III)

Over the years, the name *Sufi* has experienced a similar fate to that of Rumi's elephant. It is said that it first came into usage among the Islamic people about 150 years after the Prophet. Four hundred years later the Persian Sufi, al-Hujwiri, wrote: 'The true meaning of this name has been much discussed and many books composed on the subject'. (*Kashf al-Mahjub*, 30) The meaning of the name continues to be much discussed today, although the current explanations generally differ very little from those given by Hujwiri around 1,000 years ago in his *Kashf al-Mahjub* ('The Revelation of the Veiled'), one of the earliest Persian treatises on the Sufis.

The most common explanation given for the name *Sufi* is that it derives from the Arabic *suf* (meaning 'wool'), after the simple woollen robe *(jama'i suf)*, which, according to some, was worn by the early Islamic mystics in imitation of Christian monks and hermits. These garments, made of coarse wool sometimes mixed with horse or camel hair, were worn next to the skin and were the traditional 'hair shirt' favoured by ascetics.

Another suggested derivation is the word *saf* ('line' or 'row'), a possible reference to those early Muslims who physically positioned themselves in the first row or rank *(saff-i awwal)* for prayer or holy war. It could also refer to those who, even today, press fervently forward on the Way of Truth – the spiritually *foremost* – as opposed to 'those who stay behind'. (Qur'an 4:95) In fact this derivation forms part of a hierarchy of values established in the Qur'an, which, according to Martin Lings, 'can serve as a criterion for putting everything in its proper place. It does not only distinguish between right and wrong, orthodoxy and error, truth and falsehood and religion and paganism. It also makes a distinction, within the domain of [Islamic] orthodoxy, between those who press eagerly forward, the *foremost*, and those who observe a certain moderation in their worship . . . ' (Martin Lings, *What is Sufism?*, 30–31)

Yet another suggestion is that the name comes from *suffa*, a word used to describe the 'bench' or 'veranda' at the entrance to the mosque of the Prophet in Medina. His followers who gathered there came to be known as the *Ahl-i Suffa* (People of the Bench *or* Veranda). These impoverished early Muslims, who acknowledged their total dependence on God, have been referred to as *al-fuqara* (the poor), after the saying in the Qur'an: 'God is the Rich and ye are the poor.' The singular of *al-fuqara* is *faqir*, in Persian *darvish* (from which come our 'fakir' and 'dervish'), words frequently used by the Sufis to describe themselves.

According to Hujwiri, some people claim that the name derives from *safa* (purity), a quality epitomized in the ritual ablutions practised by Muslims. Other commentators suggest that it is derived from the Arabic verb *safwe* and means 'those who are selected'. Yet others have linked it to the Greek *sophia* (wisdom) and to *Ain Sof* (the absolutely infinite), a term from the Cabbala, the Jewish mystical tradition. (Idries Shah, *The Way of the Sufi*, 15)

Hujwiri concludes his comments about the derivation of the word *Sufi* by stating that 'the name has no derivation answering to etymological requirements . . . [And] since "Sufi" admits of no explanation, all the world are interpreters thereof, whether they recognize the dignity of the name or no at the time when they learn its meaning'. (Hujwiri, *Kashf al-Mahjub*, 34)

In other words, like Rumi's story about the elephant, our attempts to explain the meaning of the word *Sufi* are little more than our own interpretations of it. If we look back at the interpretations just given, however, we can begin to put together a picture from people's impressions of who or what 'a Sufi' is: the 'woollen robe' of the ascetic; in the 'front rank' of those on the Way of Truth; a 'close follower' of the Prophet; the 'poor'; the 'pure'; the 'selected'; and the non-Arabic words for 'wisdom' and the 'absolutely infinite'. To complete the picture, Hujwiri provides us with a concise definition: 'He that is purified by love is pure, and he that is absorbed in the Beloved and has abandoned all else is a "Sufi".' (Hujwiri, *Kashf al-Mahjub*, 34)

The '-ism' associated with the Sufis is 'Sufism' (or 'Sufi-ism' as some prefer to call it). The original word in Arabic is *tasawwuf*, which is translated as 'mysticism' and 'esoterism' as well as 'Sufism'. Hujwiri divides those who practise *tasawwuf* into three kinds:

The Sufi	practises *safa* (purity); has died to the 'self' and lives according to the Way of Truth; having broken free from the grip of his or her human faculties, he/she has attained union with the Godhead.
The Mutasawwif	seeks to become a Sufi by modelling him/herself on the example of the Sufis.
The Mustaswif	is one who imitates the Sufis for the sake of personal gain, be it for power, money, or worldly advantage, but has no knowledge of *tasawwuf*.

Like many Sufis, Hujwiri is extremely conscious of our human tendency to name things and then, having named them, to confuse the name with the reality. He quotes the tenth century Sufi Abu 'l-Hasan Fushanji as saying:

'Today *tasawwuf* is a name without a reality, but formerly it was a reality without a name.' Hujwiri adds: 'In the time of the Companions of the Prophet and their immediate successors this name did not exist, but its reality was in everyone. Now the name exists without the reality.' (Hujwiri, *Kashf al-Mahjub*, 44)

'Now the name exists without the reality' is perhaps aimed at the scholars and jurists – those whom Sayyid Amuli described as remaining on the riverbank (*see above*, page 49), for Sufis are frequently scornful of those who know the name but have no direct experience of the reality. Jalaluddin Rumi mocks those who prefer the name to the reality thus:

> Do you know a name without a thing answering to it?
> Have you ever plucked a rose from R, O, S, E?
> You name His name; go, seek the reality named by it!
> Look for the moon in the sky, not in the water!
> If you desire to rise above mere names and letters,
> Make yourself free from self at one stroke.
> Become pure from all attributes of self,
> That you may see your own bright essence,
> Yea, see in your own heart the knowledge of the Prophet,
> Without book, without tutor, without preceptor.

A Brief History of the Sufis

The first Sufis

Hujwiri's statement, 'the reality of *tasawwuf* was in everyone', is significant, for he is saying that not only were the Prophet and his Companions the first Muslims but they were also mystics – and the first Sufis in all but name. Indeed, according to a Tradition, one of the Companions is reported as saying that he had acquired two kinds of knowledge from the Prophet: the one he had taught publicly, but if he had dared to teach the other his audience would put him to death. In other words, the Prophet taught his Companions a mystical or esoteric knowledge that was not appropriate for everyone to know.

The idea of two kinds of knowledge – the one exoteric, the other esoteric – fits in with the Sufis' references to the inner and outer worlds. As we have seen, the two worlds are essentially one for the Sufis who have freed themselves from duality. Those of us who have not yet attained this unified or nondualistic state of consciousness will also see the two worlds as one, but we will see the outer world only, not the inner. The *raison d'être* of the Sufi Path is to awaken us to the inner world and the 'apprehension of divine realities', so that our consciousness may be transformed. Yet the process has certain risks.

Exposure to higher truths when one is unprepared for it leads to the interpretation of those truths from a purely exoteric viewpoint, and *in extremis* to the fanaticism associated with religious fundamentalism. (This holds true for all of the world's religious and spiritual traditions.) Because of these risks, aspirants on the Sufi Path – the 'poor' or 'dervishes' as they are known – entrust the process of their spiritual awakening to a *shaykh* (a spiritual master or teacher) who, in return, oversees his pupils' spiritual well-being and evolution towards awakening. The Sufis claim that the Prophet was the first Sufi shaykh, for the shaykhs who established the Sufi Orders (or 'Paths'; in Arabic *turuq*, plural of *tariqah*) in the centuries following the death of the Prophet trace their lineage back to him. (*see below*, The Sufi Orders, page 68) Without the guidance of a spiritual master – that is, someone (male or female) who has completed the Path themselves and is fully awakened – we can easily be led astray by our lower self, or by our own interpretation of higher truths, and thus wander off the 'Straight Path' referred to in the Fatihah. It is also possible to be led astray by false teachers, or those who falsely claim to have completed the Path.

The passing of the four 'Rightly-Guided' caliphs and the death of Imam Husayn in 680 had precipitated a parting of the ways in several different senses. There was a partial return to pre-Islamic ways, at least among those who had embraced Islam for the sake of expediency or to benefit from the spoils of war. There was also the disagreement between Sunni and Shi'i over the rightful leadership of the community. Although the caliph was nominally the spiritual leader of Islam, the three aspects of authority that had been united in the Prophet – the legal, theological, and mystical – now became divided between the jurists, the theologians, and the mystics. Essentially these three fell into two camps – the jurists and theologians, and the mystics – which reflected the exoteric and esoteric aspects of Islam. The two camps were guided respectively by the *'ulama'* (the religious authorities) and the Sufi shaykhs. Without the strong presence of the latter, the *'ulama'* would have gained unique control of the Islamic tradition and would have imposed their legalistic and religious authority in whatever way they saw fit. They might even have created an overall religious authority for the Islamic community, similar to the position held by the Vatican within Western Christianity prior to the Protestant Reformation. Professor Danner describes what would have happened if this had been the case.

> The Islamic religion would have reduplicated the same monopolistic tendencies we find in the official hierarchy of early Christianity; the latter had crushed all movements that attempted to go beyond its magisterium. A number of valid Christian gnostic teachings were thereby eradicated on the score that they belonged to the suspected heretical domain of Gnosticism. From that time on, the Church was always on its guard against any gnostic leanings among its mystics. In the Muslim world, no such effective monopoly over the contents of revelation was permitted the *'ulama'* by the Sufis. Often, the Sufis speak of the exoteric authorities (*'ulama' az-zahir*) as having a limited view of the Scripture because they tend to reject the symbolic content of revelation, or the spiritual realities embedded in the words of the text. The limitation of exoterism is thus in the mind of the exoterist . . . [and] the limitations intrinsic to the guardians of the Law cannot but influence their view of things. Whatever might be their piety, their virtuous dispositions, their religious erudition, and their noble aspirations, the religious authorities of Islam have a constricted vision of the Islamic message. (Victor Danner, *The Islamic Tradition*, 92)

In brief, the *'ulama'* concerned themselves with the outer law (*shari'ah*) while the Sufis tended the inner path (*tariqah*), the 'mystical heart of Islam', guiding the development of the religion (and the Islamic community) from within. This was a spiritual duty that the Sufis could not (and still cannot) avoid, but the way in which they manifested their guidance differed according to circumstances. Whereas exoteric religious, political, and social authorities tend to create monolithic structures that need an ever-increasing number of laws to maintain some semblance of stability, Sufis are not attached to outward form. It is the essence which is important.

Outward form belongs to the phenomenal world. As such it is transient, and so is its semblance of stability. The Sufis know that the outward forms taken by their teaching, their beliefs, and their organizations are transient too. This has precipitated the criticism that Sufis change their beliefs according to the direction in which the spiritual wind of the time is blowing. Nothing could be further from the truth. Criticism such as this comes from those who judge the Sufis according to outward appearances. The reality behind outward appearances was expressed succinctly by Ibn 'Arabi (d.1240): 'The Sufi must act and speak in a manner which takes into consideration the understanding, limitations and dominant concealed prejudices of his audience.' The outward form adopted by Sufi teaching therefore changes so that it is presented in such a way that its audience can comprehend it. Sometimes the methods appear subtle, sometimes confrontational. It all depends on which method is most appropriate for a particular audience in a particular place at a particular time. Once it has served its purpose, the outer form adapts itself to suit new circumstances.

The eighth century

By the time Rabi'ah al-'Adawiyyah of Basra was born (in around 717), a generation or more after the death of Imam Husayn, the spiritual climate was very different to what it had been at the time of the Companions of the Prophet. One of the most famous of the 'friends of God' (the Islamic equivalent of the Christian 'saint'), she was born at a time when the power of the 'Ummayad dynasty was at its height – its territory comprised the largest empire the world had ever seen. Territorial expansion coincided with a decline in spiritual awareness, however. Against this background, Rabi'ah spoke out more boldly than her predecessors, urging people to surrender the existence of their lower self to Allah with a directness that knew no compromise. She was also one of the first Sufis to give ecstatic voice to the theme of Divine

Love, a theme that was later to find its highest form of expression in the writings of the Persian poets of the twelfth and thirteenth centuries. The Sufis of the eighth century were also renowned for their humility and asceticism, perhaps none more so than the Prince of Balkh, Ibrahim ibn Adham (d.782). (For more on Rabi'ah, Ibrahim ibn Adham and the majority of the Sufis referred to in this and the following sections, *see* Chapters 6 and 7.)

Intoxication and sobriety

The conquest of new lands in the seventh and eighth centuries produced an influx of converts to Islam, many of whom brought with them elements of other religious beliefs and traditions. Some attempts were made to graft these on to Islam, resulting in the emergence of several heresies which were dealt with by the religious authorities. Having become more powerful in the second half of the eighth century under the 'Abbasid rulers, the *'ulama'* were on their guard against further heresies and eyed the Sufis with suspicion. Things came to a head in the ninth century with the emergence of what is often referred to as the 'intoxicated school' – also known as the 'drunken', 'inebriated' or 'ecstatic' Sufis. Yet this is not so much a 'school' in the conventional sense but a term used to refer to those Sufis, such as Bayazid al-Bistami (d.875/7) who, in moments of ecstatic union with the Divine, delivered inspired utterances which could be taken as blasphemous. For the exoteric *'ulama'*, the 'ecstatic' Sufis were heretics. None more so than al-Hallaj who was tried and condemned for blasphemy, but not executed until several years later in 922.

Hallaj had at one time studied under Junayd (d.910), a leading member of the Sufi fraternity in Baghdad. Junayd was of the opinion that the esoteric knowledge of the Sufis was not for everyone and he had consequently warned Hallaj and several of his other pupils about speaking too freely in front of those who would misunderstand their intentions. Because he advocated a more restrained approach than that adopted by the ecstatics, Junayd is often described as the head of the 'sober school' of Sufis.

Early writings of the Sufis

The tenth century saw a proliferation of textbooks and treatises by Sufis, which were written with the intention of avoiding further misunderstanding and confrontation with the religious authorities. Among these authors were Abu Nasr al-Sarraj of Tus (d.988), whose *Kitab al-Luma'* ('Book of Brilliancies') is said to be the earliest surviving treatise on Sufism; Abu Talib al-Makki, whose *Qut al-Qulub* ('The Nourishment of Hearts') set out to reconcile Sufism with orthodox Islam; Abu Bakr al-Kalabadhi (d.c.1000), whose *al-Ta'arruf li-madhhab ahl al-tasauwuf* ('The Doctrine of the Sufis') is described by A. J. Arberry, its translator, as 'more frankly apologetic than his predecessors' works'; Abu 'Abd al-Rahman al-Sulami (d.1021), author of *Tabaqat al-Sufiya*, a collection of biographies of the Sufis; Abu 'l-Qasim al-Qushairi of Nishapur (d.1072), whose *Risala* was a concise summary of Sufism; and 'Ali ibn 'Uthman al-Hujwiri (d.1074), author of *Kashf al-Mahjub* ('Revelation of the Veiled'), one of the oldest Sufi works in Persian.

The figure who possibly did more than anyone else to bridge the divide between orthodox Islam and the Sufis – between the Law (*shari'ah*) and the Path (*tariqah*) – was Abu Hamid al-Ghazali (d.1111). His writings served to return Sufism to its rightful place as a continuation of the original mystical heart of Islam. The most important of Ghazali's works in this connection is considered to be the *Ihya' 'ulum ad-din* ('The Revival of the Religious Sciences'). His autobiographical *al-Munqidh min ad-Dalal* ('Deliverance from Error') recounts his personal spiritual crisis and subsequent search for the true essence of religion, which he found among the Sufis.

The Persian poets

Arabic was the language of the Qur'an and the first language of Islam, but in the twelfth century there was a flowering of the use of Persian poetry as a vehicle for expounding Sufi teaching. The basic verse forms used were the *qasida* (formal ode), *ghazal* (lyric), *ruba'i* (quatrain) and *mathnawi* (rhyming couplet), while the term *divan* was used for a collection of poetry.

Perhaps the most widely known work of Persian Sufi poetry is the *Rubaiyat* (a collection of quatrains) of Omar Khayyam (a mathematician, scientist, and philosopher), thanks to Edward Fitzgerald's nineteenth century English translation. Hakim Sana'i (d.c.1150) is considered to have been the first to break new ground by using the traditional *mathnawi* for spiritual instruction in his *Hadiqat al-haqiqah* ('Garden of the Truth'). He was followed by Fariduddin Attar (1142–1220/1229) in his *Mantiq al-tair* ('Conference of the Birds') and other works, and Jalaluddin Rumi (1207–1273) in his *Masnavi-i-Ma'navi* ('Spiritual Couplets'), better known simply as the *Mathnawi*. (These are extensive works: Attar's *Conference of the Birds* comprises some 5,000 couplets, while Rumi's *Mathnawi* has over 25,000 verses.) Sa'di of Shiraz (d.1292) is noted for his *Bustan* ('Fruit Garden' or 'Orchard'), and his *Gulistan* ('Rose Garden'), which are combinations of verse and prose (stories, anecdotes, aphorisms, etc.), written in a simple, timeless language that has succeeded in embedding his work, and its Sufi content, in Persian popular culture. The 'garden' has long been associated with the original Edenic Paradise, the state in which human beings are in harmony with both the Creation and the Creator (the outer and inner worlds respectively). As such, it is an appropriate title for Sufi writings that offer guidance on the path by which we may return to this state. Shabistari (1250–1320) used it for his *Gulshan i Raz* ('Secret Rose Garden'). The Persian Sufi poetic tradition continued into the fourteenth century with Hafiz of Shiraz (d.1389) and into the fifteenth with Jami (1414–1492), who is considered to have been the last of the great Sufi poets.

The Sufi Orders

The Sufi Orders, which began to appear in the tenth century, are not to be confused with the monastic orders of Christianity. The latter are closed or semi-closed monastic orders, whereas the Arabic word that translates as 'Order' into English is *tariqah*, which we encountered earlier in the context of its alternative meaning of the inner or spiritual path. The Sufi Orders are more in the nature of brotherhoods which gather around a shaykh or spiritual master. When the Prophet was alive, his close followers sat around him in circles to receive his teaching. Because this was part of the Prophetic Sunnah, the same system was adopted by later generations of Muslims. It was also used by the Sufi shaykhs. Prior to the existence of the *tariqah*, the shaykh would sit and instruct his followers in any available corner: his home, a garden, a courtyard, a mosque or a cave. When the *tariqah*s became more institutionalized they moved into a purpose-built meeting-house known as a *zawiyah* (literally 'corner'), *khanaqah* in Persian and *tekke* in Turkish. Whereas the purpose of the *zawiyah* was instruction in the Path (the esoteric aspect of Islam), the Law (the exoteric aspect) was taught in religious schools known as *madrasahs*.

The Sufi *tariqah*s arose naturally when a group of followers began to gather around a particular shaykh – with the passing of time the group came to be known by the name of the shaykh whose teaching it followed. For example, the *tariqah* that formed around Shaykh Abd al-Qadir al-Jilani (d.1166) in Baghdad became known as the *Qadiriyyah* or Qadiri Order. Some of the principal Sufi Orders and the shaykhs from whom they take their name are: the *Chishtiyyah* or Chishti, after Mu'in ad-Din Chishti of Chisht in Afghanistan (d.1233); the *Shadhiliyyah* or Shadhili, after Shaykh Abu'l Hasan al-Shadhili of Morocco (d.1258); the *Mevleviyyah* or Mevlevi, after Mevlana Jalaluddin Rumi of Konya (d.1273); the *Bektashiyyah* or Bektashi, after Hajji Bektash of Khorasan (d.1338); and the *Naqshbandiyyah* or Naqshbandi, after Shaykh Bahaudin Naqshband of Bukhara (d.1390). When the founding shaykh died, the order continued under his successor, using the founding shaykh's name. Sometimes a new Order emerged from within an older Order. The *Darqawiyyah* or Darqawi Order, for example, which takes its name from Shaykh Mulay al-Arabi ad-Darqawi of Morocco (d.1823), was a branch of the much older Shadhili Order, founded in the thirteenth century.

As well as forming new branches, Orders would sometimes merge with each other yet whether they are direct lines, branches or mergers each Order has its own chain of transmission – the *silsilah* – which connects the shaykhs of today with the first Sufi shaykh, the Prophet Muhammad. Sufi Orders are now active in all parts of the world, although some are active on some continents and not on others. In some Orders women and men enjoy equal status.

When an order came into being it was born of a unique set of circumstances that arose from a number of variable factors: spiritual, cultural, political, social, economic and ethnic or tribal. Each Order therefore not only evolved its own unique 'flavour', but it also developed a system of practices that were best suited to its followers. It should be stressed that there is no competition between the Orders, for although their outward forms might appear different their primary concern is the *tariqah* or inner Path of awakening. As Shaykh Fadhlalla Haeri says: ' *'Ulama'* (religious authorities) have traditionally sought outer uniformity while experiencing inner disunity, whereas the Sufis seek inner unity while tolerating outer differences.' (Shaykh Fadhlalla Haeri, *Elements of Islam*, 70)

The Golden Age and after

With justifiable reason, the twelfth and thirteenth centuries are sometimes considered to have been the Golden Age of Sufism. It was an age that began with Ghazali (d.1111) and the integration of Sufi principles at the heart of Islam; it witnessed the flowering of Persian poetry as a vehicle for Sufi teaching in the work of Attar (d.1220/9), Rumi (d.1273) and Sa'di (d.1292); it gave birth to the great Sufi Orders of the Qadiri, Chishti, Shadhili and others; and it was the age of the great Sufi masters Jalaluddin Rumi and Muhyiddin Ibn 'Arabi (d.1240), whose prolific writings have had an influence on Sufi thought ever since.

Nowadays, the description of a particular historical period as a 'Golden Age' implies nostalgia, a desire to return to an earlier time. But this is not the case with the Sufis, unless it is the intrinsic desire of the drop to return to the ocean from whence it came. Then again, if we look back to the Sufi masters of this period it is perhaps in the spirit expressed by a Christian contemporary, Bernard of Chartres (d.c.1130):

> We are like dwarfs on the shoulders of giants, so that we can see more than they, and things at a greater distance, not by virtue of any sharpness of sight on our part, or any physical distinction, but because we are carried high and raised up by their giant size.

By the fourteenth century, Sufism (*tasawwuf*) had become an integral part of Islam, as is apparent from the following words of Taj ad-Din as-Subki, a jurist of the period. He sets out the 'sciences of religion' in the following formulation; his mention of 'the Tradition reported by the son of 'Umar' is a reference to the *hadith* reported by the Caliph 'Umar, quoted in Chapter 3 under '*Iman*, *Islam*, and *Ihsan*'.

> The sciences of the religion are three: jurisprudence (*fiqh*) which is referred to in the Tradition reported by the son of 'Umar as *islam* (submission), the theological principles (*usul ad-din*), which are referred to as *iman* (faith), and mysticism (*tasawwuf*) which is referred to as *ihsan* (excellence). As to anything else, it must either be reduced to one of these denominations, or otherwise it is outside the religion.
>
> (Martin Lings, *What is Sufism?*, 116)

If the more overt divisions between religious authorities and Sufis – *shari'ah* and *tariqah* (Law and Path) – had been resolved, the same could not be said of the divisions between outer and inner realities. Each generation has to face in its own way the apparent separation of the individual human being from the Divine Unity and the concomitant resistance of the will of the lower self to the Divine Will. In a letter written to his disciples, Shaykh al-'Arabi ad-Darqawi (d.1823) describes the situation in his own time. His words have a timeless ring of truth that makes them equally relevant to the twenty-first century.

> Our attention should be devoted to religious activity at all times and today more than ever, for in these days one might well imagine that no such thing as religious activity without worldly attachment had ever existed; nevertheless it certainly has existed even if it exists no longer . . . We observe (but God knows best) that in these days no one is able to say to the multitude of believers: 'reduce your worldly activities and increase your religious activities; God will replace you (in your business) as He has done for others.' Today nobody will listen to you – and God knows best – unless you say: 'cultivate (your fields), earn, trade' and so forth. But if you say: 'leave it, abstain (from the world) and be content,' there are very few, even among the elect who will listen to you – the others even less.
>
> (Shaykh al-'Arabi ad-Darqawi, *Letters of a Sufi Master*, 31–32)

The last two sentences are especially relevant to an age whose vocabulary is dominated by talk of the global economy, world trade and market forces. But outwardly things are never quite what they seem to be.

The Sufis and the West

In what can be only the briefest of summaries, it is safe to say that the Sufis have exerted a subtle but considerable influence on Western culture since the beginning of the eighth century, when the 'Ummayad armies conquered most of Spain and Muslims settled in the Iberian Peninsula. The architectural legacy of the period that followed is evident in the Moorish citadel-palace of the Alhambra (from the Arabic *al-hamra*, meaning 'red', because of the colour of the fortified wall surrounding it) in Granada and in the pointed arch, the architectural feature that made possible the soaring cathedrals of the Gothic period. The Alhambra was begun in 1238, two years before the death of Ibn 'Arabi (d.1240), known as *Shaykh al-Akbar* ('the Great Master'), who left a legacy of a different kind in his prolific writings. Sufi influence also came to Europe with the return of the Crusaders and the writings of Sufis such as Fariduddin Attar (d.c.1220/1229), whose *Conference of the Birds* inspired some of Chaucer's *Canterbury Tales* and gave the Swiss the legend of William Tell. Chaucer had been dead for almost a hundred years when the Spanish reconquest of Granada in 1492 brought an end to the Sufi-inspired Spanish Arabic civilization.

Archaeological digs in the Middle and Near East during the nineteenth century prompted a revival of interest in the artistic and religious culture of the region. The work of Orientalists and scholars – Sir Richard Burton, Edward Fitzgerald, E. H. Whinfield, R. A. Nicholson and others – made translations of Arabic and Persian texts available to an ever-widening public and, in the process, gave greater access to Sufi materials hitherto unpublished in English. All of this prepared the ground for the Sufi teachers who were to travel westwards in the twentieth century.

The first of these was Hazrat Inayat Khan (1882–1927) who, in 1910, travelled by sea from Bombay to New York. His purpose in making this journey was 'to bring a message of Sufism, of inner wisdom, to the world, harmonizing East and West . . . In doing this he modernized the age-old Sufi wisdom and made it universal, so that it could emerge from the Islamic context in which it had developed for centuries.' (H. J. Witteveen, *Universal Sufism*, xi) To this end he established the Sufi Movement and the Universal Worship, which brings the world's great religions together in a single act of worship. This simple ritual comprises readings from the sacred writings of the major religions and the lighting of a candle for each religion to symbolize the transmission of the divine light to humanity. The work of Hazrat Inayat Khan in the West is continued by his two sons, Pir Vilayat Inayat Khan, head of the Sufi Order International, and Pir-o-Murshid Hidayat Inayat Khan, head of the Sufi Movement.

In the latter part of the twentieth century Shaykh Muzaffer Ozak (1916–1986) made more than twenty journeys to Europe and the USA, initiating many hundreds into the Halveti-Jerrahi Order of which he was the spiritual head. He taught in numerous mosques in Istanbul, his birthplace, and during his lifetime was acknowledged as one of the few great living Sufi teachers. When asked about the near total destruction of the Sufi Orders in Turkey in the 1920s by Kamal Ataturk, he replied with a smile: 'You look upon it as destruction. We look upon it as slightly excessive grooming . . . It is like chopping a grapevine to the ground. If he had chopped a little, the branches would have grown only a few metres away, but because he cut the whole grapevine to the ground, it will now grow all over the place. It is only a matter of time.' (Shaykh Fadhlalla Haeri, *The Elements of Sufism*, 77–78)

Shaykh Muzaffer's words have since come true. In the last fifty years, many thousands of Westerners have been initiated into the various Sufi Orders by shaykhs who have travelled to the West. Among these are Shaykh Fadhlalla Haeri, Shaykh Hakim Moinuddin Chishti, Shaykh Nazim 'Adl al-Haqqani and the late Shaykh Suleyman Dede. In the same period the writings of Idries Shah, Titus Burckhardt, Frithjof Schuon and many others have also done much to promote Sufi ideas in the West. Two books in particular by Idries Shah, *The Way of the Sufi* and *The Sufis*, both written in the 1960s, have introduced Sufi ideas and the Sufi way of learning to many thousands of Westerners. Indeed, Western interest in the inner way of the Sufis has never been greater.

This brings us back to an issue referred to in the Introduction to this book, which will no doubt continue to be a matter of debate. Is it possible to be a Sufi without Islam? In this, as in everything else, Allah knows best.

Chapter Five:

Sufi Symbolism

In this chapter we take a brief look at some of the powerful symbolic imagery employed by the Sufis in their writings and teachings on the Divine Unity (*tawhid*). Symbols are a useful means of understanding how outer and inner realities are fused together, because symbolism starts with the premise that a symbolic object (the outer reality) has an underlying meaning (its inner reality). Problems seem to arise, however, when we try to apply the same principle to our everyday lives (the outer reality) and their underlying meaning or purpose (the inner reality). We tend to look for meaning and purpose in our lives in terms of the outer reality, as though they are somewhere 'out there' – in the future or in another place – rather than being right here where we are. If you think about it for a moment, when we look at a symbol we perceive its inner meaning at the same time that we perceive the outer reality. The outer form is simply a veil that separates us from the inner reality.

The advantage of an established vocabulary of symbols such as that used by the Sufis is that once we are aware of the symbolic meaning we no longer need to use our analytical mind to work it out. Thus freed from reliance upon the outer form, the inner reality of the symbol can speak directly to us. The veil of separation has been removed.

The examples of thematic imagery we will look at here are: the drop and the ocean; the wine of the Beloved; and the lover and the Beloved. These are followed by two classic love stories – Joseph and Zulaikha and Layla and Majnun – which are frequently alluded to in the writings of the Sufis.

The Drop and the Ocean

The natural cycle by which water from the ocean evaporates, falls on the land as rain and then makes its way along streams and rivers back to the ocean is used as a metaphor for the journey of the individual human soul back to union with its Source. Hence the many Sufi references to the drop becoming one with the ocean, to drowning, swimming, fish and pearls.

Drop of water	the individual human being
Fish	the individual human being
Ocean	the Divine Unity
Pearl	an enlightened or fully realized human being

When the drop departed from its native home and returned,
It found a shell and became a pearl. (From the *Divani Shamsi Tabriz*)

A single drop of rain fell from a cloud in the sky,
But was filled with shame when it saw the sea so wide.
'Next to the sea then, who am I?
If the sea exists, then how can I?'

While looking down on itself
With the eyes of contempt,
An oyster in its shell,
Took it in for nourishment.

And so it was, that its fate was sealed by this event,
And it became a famous pearl fit to adore a king's head.
Having descended to the depths,
It was now exalted to the heights.
On the portal of non-existence it went knocking,
Until it finally was transformed into being. (From the *Bustan* of Sa'di)

All know that the drop merges into the ocean but few know that the ocean merges into the drop.

(Kabir, d.1518)

The Wine of the Beloved

Unless we have been forewarned about the symbolic language of the Sufis we could easily assume that poets such as Omar Khayyam (d.*c*.1123) or Hafiz (d.1390), spent most of their time in a drunken stupor. Or if they were not writing about being drunk, they were looking forward to getting drunk. Such an assumption is easy to make if we take the poetry at face value and ignore its symbolic function. It also serves to underline the point that the Sufi poets are writing about something that is beyond the understanding of most of us. They are writing about a different state of consciousness: one that is as radically different from a normal state of sobriety as being high on drugs or alcohol. For the Sufis, it is the different state of consciousness that is important. The alcoholic imagery is not only secondary but it is also a metaphor for the spiritual ecstasy experienced in moments of profound union with the Divine. (*see* Chapter 4, Intoxication and sobriety, page 66) Some of the meanings behind the symbolic imagery are:

Cup bearer	the person who serves wine, and whose attention one seeks to gain in order to be served: metaphor for the Sufi shaykh, or for Allah.
Drunkard	a person who is intoxicated and no longer has control over his/her actions: the ecstatic Sufi.
Drunkenness	intoxication, or an altered state of consciousness: spiritual ecstasy.
Tavern	a place to which a drunkard goes to drink and get drunk:the spiritual heart of the individual, where he/she can imbibe the wine of Divine Love.

Tavern haunter	a drunkard, someone in a permanent state of inebriation: the Sufi who has freed him/herself from the lower self.
Wine	forbidden to his followers by the Prophet, but promised to the faithful in Paradise: spiritual ecstasy; communion with the Divine; knowledge of the Divine; the Divine Love which fills the cup of the mystic's heart.
Wine-seller	like the cup-bearer, someone who serves wine: a spiritual guide (*shaykh* or *pir*).

You know, my Friends, with what a brave Carouse
I made a Second Marriage in my house;
Divorced old barren Reason from my Bed,
And took the Daughter of the Vine to Spouse.
(From the *Rubaiyat* of Omar Khayyam, tr. Edward Fitzgerald)

And lately, by the Tavern Door agape,
Came stealing through the Dusk an Angel Shape
Bearing a Vessel on his Shoulder; and
He bid me taste of it; and 'twas – the Grape!
(*Rubaiyat* of Omar Khayyam)

Self, Hafiz, self! That must thou overcome!
Hearken the wisdom of the tavern-daughter!
Vain little baggage – well, upon my word!
Thou fairy figment made of clay and water,
As busy with thy beauty as a bird.
Well, Hafiz, life's a riddle – give it up:
There is no answer to it but this cup.
(Hafiz, quoted in H. J. Witteveen, *Universal Sufism*, 13)

The Lover and the Beloved

In the same way that poems celebrating spiritual intoxication can be taken to be little more than drinking songs, poems written in celebration of Divine Love can be mistaken for erotic poetry. Such was the case for Ibn Arabi, who was accused of writing licentious poems to celebrate the charms of Nizam, the daughter of a Sufi shaykh (*see* page 165). To refute the charge he provided a written commentary on some of his poems. A few lines from one of the poems follow the brief vocabulary of some of the symbolism associated with the love poetry of the Sufis. It will be noted that Ibn Arabi's lines combine the symbolic imagery of the Beloved with that of the Ocean. The poem is followed by the classic love stories of Joseph and Zulaikha, and Layla and Majnun.

Beauty	the Glory of the Beloved.
Down (on the cheek)	the world of spiritual forms – that is to say, the world which is nearest to the Divine, or the Face of God.
Embraces/Kisses	love's ecstatic raptures.
Face/Cheek	the Face of God, which reveals its Divine Beauty through its Attributes/Names.
Hair/Curls & Tresses	the world of multiplicity veiling the face of Unity.
Mole (on the cheek)	the dot under the Arabic letter 'ba' (بْ) and the Unity of Knowledge symbolized by the point/dot (see Chapter 2, The Qur'an, page 35).
Perfume	a blessing (*baraqah*); the invisible Presence of God.

Oh, her beauty – the tender maid! Its brilliance gives light
  like lamps to one travelling in the dark.
She is a pearl hidden in a shell of hair as black as jet,
A pearl for which Thought dives and remains unceasingly
  in the deeps of that ocean.
He who looks upon her deems her to be a gazelle of the sand-hills,
  because of her shapely neck and the loveliness of her gestures. (Ibn Arabi)

Joseph and Zulaikha (Yusuf and Zulaykha)

An entire chapter of the Qur'an (Surah 12) is dedicated to the story of Joseph, Jacob's son, who is regarded as a prophet by Muslims. The main elements of the story are very similar to those told in the biblical Book of Genesis – Joseph's jealous brothers, his slavery in Egypt, his master's wife's attempted seduction of him, his imprisonment, his rise to a position of power in the land and his reconciliation with his father and brothers. (Genesis 37–50) But one element in particular is different in the story as it is retold: the woman known simply as Potiphar's wife in Genesis, and who remains unnamed in the Qur'an, is now named Zulaikha. Two episodes in the Qur'anic version of the story – Zulaikha's attempted seduction of Joseph and her wily ruse for silencing the ensuing gossip – form the basis of the classic love story that has been told and retold ever since.

Tradition relates that Joseph was the most handsome youth who ever lived and when Zulaikha first set eyes on her husband's new slave she fell deeply in love: so deeply in love that she was the one enslaved. Her thoughts were for Joseph alone. In her desire for him, she showered him with expensive gifts, and made suggestive advances, but Joseph remained impervious to her charms. For him, loyalty to his master was paramount. One day, however, Zulaikha lured Joseph to her apartment in a determined effort to seduce him. When Joseph fled from her embrace she grabbed him by his shirt, tearing it as he left the room. As they raced through the door they ran into Zulaikha's husband, who happened to be passing his wife's apartment at that moment. To explain away her unusual conduct – racing through her rooms after a slave was not considered appropriate behaviour for the wife of the Vizier – Zulaikha immediately accused Joseph of having tried to rape her. The Vizier investigated the affair: when it was discovered that Joseph's shirt had been torn from behind it was evident that he had been trying to run away. If he had been the attacker, as Zulaikha claimed, his shirt would have been torn from the front. The Vizier declared Joseph innocent, but a question mark remained over his wife's behaviour. Rather than run the risk of causing a scandal, he decided to leave the matter there.

Not so Zulaikha. She continued to behave towards Joseph in such a scandalous way that her conduct soon became the subject of society gossip. When she learned that her women friends were talking about her behind her back, accusing her of having an illicit affair with her slave, Zulaikha decided to get even with them. She invited them all to lunch and served them oranges for dessert, along with a very sharp knife to remove the peel. While her guests were peeling their fruit, she sent for Joseph. When he entered the room, they all looked up and were so captivated by his beauty that they were unable to take their eyes off him. They forgot what they were doing and ended up by cutting their fingers so badly that they eventually came to their senses. 'Do you blame me now?' asked Zulaikha.

Having been themselves spellbound by Joseph's beauty, Zulaikha's guests became sympathetic to her situation. They advised her to threaten Joseph with prison unless he returned her love. She sent for Joseph, but his response to her threats was not what she had hoped to hear, for he said that he would rather go to prison for the rest of his life than be disloyal to his master by succumbing to her demands. Frustrated by the object of her desire, Zulaikha persuaded her husband to have Joseph sent to prison.

Many years later the Pharaoh sent for Joseph, having heard of his reputation as an interpreter of dreams. He hoped that Joseph could reveal the meaning of some unusual dreams that he had been experiencing. Joseph took the opportunity to protest his innocence and refused to attend the Pharaoh until he had been set free. The Pharaoh re-opened Joseph's case. He sent for Zulaikha's women friends, who said that Joseph had always behaved nobly and respectfully towards them. As for Zulaikha, her heart had been opened by her love for Joseph and she now confessed that her lies had sent an innocent man to prison. Without further ado, the Pharaoh had Joseph released. Impressed by his many qualities, he appointed him to the post of Vizier which had become vacant following the death of Zulaikha's husband.

More years passed during which Joseph and Zulaikha went their separate ways. Joseph became rich and powerful: the second most powerful man in the land, after the Pharaoh. At first Zulaikha had given away her precious jewels to anyone who brought her news of Joseph, but her jewels had long since gone. Now she was reduced to begging in the streets, dressed in the ragged remains of her once fine clothes. Time had eroded her beauty, too.

One day, while riding through the city surrounded by his entourage, Joseph caught sight of a small crowd that had assembled by the roadside. He sent one of his guards to find out the reason for the gathering.

'It's some poor beggar,' said the guard when he returned. 'She's collapsed.'

Aware of the Vizier's presence, the crowd drew aside. Joseph looked long and hard at the beggar lying on the ground: there was something vaguely familiar about her. A memory from long ago came to him. He dismounted and, kneeling beside her, said: 'Zulaikha, is it really you?'

At the sound of his voice, she opened her eyes. Joseph looked into them and saw that they were filled with light. The outer beauty of her youth may have faded, but it had given way to a radiant inner beauty that shone through her outer form. Joseph spoke again: 'You once loved me, Zulaikha, with a love that I was unable to return. I was a mere slave, and you were my master's wife. But things are different now.'

'They are,' said Zulaikha. 'My eyes have been opened. My all-consuming love for you was but a pale shadow of Divine Love, a veil between myself and the Beloved. But the veil has been torn aside. Now that I have found the Beloved, I no longer need your love.'

The ending that is given here is taken from Sheikh Muzaffer Ozak's rendering of the story of Joseph and Zulaikha in *Love is the Wine*. A different ending, and a fuller version of the story, will be found in Mojdeh Bayat and Mohammad Ali Jamnia, *Tales from the Land of the Sufis*.

Layla and Majnun

Once in Arabia there were a boy and girl who were the children of two different tribes. The boy was named Qays, while the girl was given the name Layla, meaning 'Night', because of the colour of her hair and eyes. Both children were exceedingly beautiful and from the moment they first met they only had eyes for each other. Their love was evident for all to see. Soon people began to gossip. When news of their love reached the ears of Layla's father, he confined her to the family tent and banned Qays from approaching their tribal encampment.

The distraught Qays wrote poetry for his beloved Layla, reciting it as he wandered the neighbourhood hoping to catch a glimpse of her. Intoxicated with love, his thoughts were solely for Layla. She had become his only reality. His obsession with her was such that people began to call him by another name – Majnun, meaning 'madman' – and this is the name by which we now know him.

Majnun told the birds about his love for Layla, believing that they would fly to her and tell her that he was near. He spoke to the water of a small stream that flowed through her tribe's encampment, willing it to carry his love to her. And when the wind blew from the direction of her encampment, he breathed deeply in hope of catching her scent. As for Layla, when birds flew overhead she imagined they were the bearers of Majnun's love for her. She sat for long hours by the little stream, for its bubbling noise sounded like Majnun's voice whispering her name lovingly. When the wind blew towards Majnun's encampment, she would stand so that it rippled through her silken garments and thus carry her scent to him. She wrote love poems to Majnun, too, releasing them into the air as though freeing a bird from a cage, so that the wind carried them away. Whenever people found them they took them to Majnun. In this way the lovers were to some extent able to overcome their sense of separation.

One day Majnun thought of a ruse by which he could get to see Layla. He acquired the skin of a sheep from a shepherd whom he then asked to take his flock to Layla's tribal encampment. Once there he was to drive the flock past Layla's tent while he, Majnun, would go down on all fours and hide himself among the sheep, concealed by the sheepskin. He approached her tent from the side, and when he lifted the canvas he caught sight of the hem of his beloved's skirt. But even this was too much for the lovestruck Majnun, for he fainted away. The shepherd had to carry him away from the encampment and splash cold water on his face to revive him.

Some friends met Majnun while he was still dressed only in the sheepskin.

Part One

One of them said: 'Why are you wearing that old sheepskin? Let me bring you some proper clothes.'

'There is no garment I could possibly wear that would be worthy of my beloved Layla,' replied Majnun. 'Not even the finest silk or rarest brocade. As far as I am concerned there is nothing better than this woollen fleece, which I wear for the sake of love since it enabled me to catch a glimpse of my beloved.'

On another occasion Majnun was observed sifting through the dust by the roadside, as though he had lost something. Someone asked him: 'What are you looking for?'

'I'm looking for Layla.'

'Layla is a woman. How can you hope to find her there in the dust?'

'I look for her everywhere,' replied Majnun, 'in the hope of finding her somewhere.'

Eventually Layla's father heard of Majnun's ruse with the sheepskin. He placed a guard around her tent so that any further attempt by Majnun to get close to her seemed hopeless. He withdrew into the mountains, and for a while no one heard of him. Meanwhile Layla's father consented to her marriage to another man, but her love for Majnun prevented her husband from ever getting close to her. When he died some years later she appeared genuinely grief-stricken, such was the flow of her tears. Unbeknown to others, however, her heart-rending sobs were her way of mourning the years of separation from her beloved Majnun.

Shortly afterwards, Layla fell ill. The best doctors in the land were called to her bedside, but there was nothing they could do to heal her. She slipped in and out of consciousness, and when she breathed her last it was to say 'Majnun'. When the news of her death reached her beloved, he fainted away.

One tradition relates that Majnun made his way to her tomb, over which he mourned for a few days before he too left this world. His body was discovered a year later, on the anniversary of Layla's death, and he was buried beside her so that the two were united in this world as well as in the next.

This particular ending appears in Mojdeh Bayat and Mohammad Ali Jamnia, *Tales from the Land of the Sufis*, which also contains a fuller version of the story. The shortened version given in the preceding pages is derived from various sources, including Attar's *Conference of the Birds*.

Commenting on Majnun and his relationship with Layla, an anonymous writer from the Safavid period (sixteenth to seventeenth century Persia) stated: 'I am whom I love; whom I love is me; we are two spirits immanent in a single body.' (James G. Cowan, *Where Two Oceans Meet*, 33)

At the heart of the story of Layla and Majnun lies our relationship with the Divine Essence, described by Martin Lings as 'the holiest and most secret inwardness of God' which also 'marks the end of the mystical path'. (William Stoddart, *Sufism*, 74) The Arabic word for the Divine Essence, *Dhat*, is feminine in gender, hence the goal of the Sufi path is frequently personified as a woman. The woman is usually named Layla, meaning 'night', and for the Sufis denotes the Mystery of the Divine Essence. (Martin Lings, *What is Sufism?*, 54, n21)

The woollen fleece worn by Majnun when he caught sight of his beloved, and which he then refused to exchange for another garment, can be understood as an allusion to the 'woollen robe' of the Sufi. The woollen robe of the Sufi is itself an outer symbol of his/her inner state, having 'seen' (that is, had direct experience of) the Beloved.

The final word on the story of Layla and Majnun is best left to Muhammad al-Harraq (d.1845): 'Seekest thou Layla [Divine Reality], when she is manifest within thee? Thou deemest her to be other, but she is not other than thou.' (Quoted in William Stoddart, *Sufism*, 84)

Chapter Six:

Lives of the Sufis

We have already met with the Sufis' use of stories as a teaching method. But Sufi storytelling is not confined to classic tales such as Joseph and Zulaikha, or Layla and Majnun, nor to the writings of Attar and Rumi. Events from the lives of the Sufis have themselves been transformed into anecdotal stories, often self-mocking in style, which are used to convey a specific lesson or elucidate an aspect of Sufi teaching. To Western eyes some of these stories may appear far-fetched, but if we find ourselves asking 'is this true?' or 'did this really happen?' we might be missing the real point of the story. The point could just be to show us how easily our search for deeper truths can be diverted by questions such as 'is this true?'.

The lives of the Sufis are presented here in a relatively straightforward manner. First comes a short introductory paragraph or two of what can best be described as 'conventional biography'. This is followed by a selection of anecdotal stories, of the kind described above, which tend to emphasize the characteristics for which a particular figure was renowned during his or her lifetime. Anecdotes about Rabi'ah of Basra, for example, reflect her devotional love of Allah, whereas those about Ibrahim ibn Adham, the Prince of Balkh, dwell on his extreme humility, and his renunciation of his kingdom to become a wandering dervish.

Rabi'ah and Ibrahim ibn Adham both lived in the eighth century. By the thirteenth century, the age of Jalaluddin Rumi and Ibn Arabi, documentary records had become much more common: not only of the lives of the Sufis but also of their teachings. As a consequence, there was no longer quite the same need to write the biographical anecdotes about contemporary Sufis that had been produced five centuries earlier. Besides, the wealth of stories about the earlier Sufis was such that they were retold for a different age by Rumi, Attar and other poets.

There were other changes, too. The military conquests of the seventh and eighth centuries had led to the rapid geographical expansion of the Caliphate and the spread of Islam. This expansion is mirrored in the names of the towns and cities in which Sufis were born or worked, and in the establishment of Sufi centres ever farther away (geographically speaking, at least) from Mecca and Medina: Basra and Kufa in Mesopotamia; Damascus in Syria; the Persian province of Khorasan; the new city of Baghdad (begun c.750 CE); and, beyond these, other centres in Egypt, North Africa, Spain, Afghanistan and India.

Whereas the majority of early Sufis had been Arabs, the later Sufis were of many different nationalities: Omar Khayyam, Attar, and Rumi were Persian; Ibn Arabi came from Andalusia, in Spain; and Dhu 'l-Nun was Egyptian. The range of languages used by the Sufis and those who write about them has led to considerable variations in the spelling of proper names. The spelling of names has been further complicated in that some of these languages are written down using consonants only. Their transcription necessitates the addition of vowels, which means that a choice has to be made as to which vowel best represents the sound of the spoken word. Hence the variation. The name at the head of each biography is the one most frequently encountered in literature about the Sufis. Where relevant, this is accompanied (in parentheses) by either a longer version of the name or a commonly used alternative.

The Sufis' experience of life is very different from that of most of us. Because of their self-abandonment to the Divine Unity they are no longer governed by their ego-centred will, and so they experience life from within a universal rather than a personal context. This is one reason why the personal anecdotes they tell, and the stories that are told about them, have such a universal appeal: they remind us – consciously or unconsciously – of our own profound connection with a greater, transpersonal Reality. The universal relevance of these tales means that the timeless wisdom they contain also has relevance for us personally, both in our outer everyday lives and our inner spiritual evolution.

Hasan of Basra (Hasan al-Basri: 642–728)

The son of a freed slave, Hasan was raised in Medina where he met many of the Companions of the Prophet and received the blessing of Imam 'Umar, the second Caliph. He is also said to have sat at the feet of Imam 'Ali, the fourth Caliph, and it is through Hasan that many of the Sufi *tariqah*s trace their spiritual lineage to Imam 'Ali and thus to the Prophet Muhammad. As his name implies, Hasan spent the greater part of his life in Basra and it was there that he died. During his lifetime he acquired a considerable reputation for his great piety and humility, and in classical Sufism he is sometimes referred to as one of the Four Masters or Four Guides. Of the following anecdotal stories that Hasan told about himself, the first two are typically self-deprecatory.

Hasan tells how one day he noticed a man and a woman sitting on the river bank. In front of them was a wine-skin. The scene caused Hasan to think self-righteously to himself: 'If only I could reform this degenerate wretch and make him more like me!' At that precise moment a boat out on the river began to sink, throwing seven people into the water. Without hesitation the man Hasan had been watching leapt in the river. When he had successfully rescued six of the seven people, the man went up to Hasan and said: 'Hasan, if you really are better than me, in the name of Allah save the last man.' Hasan relates that he was unable to save him, and the man drowned. The rescuer then said to Hasan: 'The woman with me is my mother, and the wine-flask is filled with water. Do you see how judgemental you have been? But then that's just the sort of person you are.' At this Hasan threw himself at the other man's feet: 'You rescued six out of the seven whose lives were in peril, save me from drowning in human pride disguised as spiritual merit!' (Idries Shah, *Thinkers of the East*, 48)

Habib al-'Ajami, Hasan's eventual successor, was Persian – 'ajami means 'Persian' – and had considerable difficulties with reciting the prayers and the Qur'an corectly because Arabic was not his native tongue. When the two men performed the ritual prayer together it was usual for Hasan, as master and the elder of the two, to lead the prayer with Habib standing behind him. On one particular occasion, however, Habib began to pray, unaware of his master's presence. Performing the ritual prayer on one's own is permissible only if there is no alternative, and so in the circumstances it would have been preferable for Hasan to position himself behind Habib and join in the prayer. But he had doubts about the validity of the prayer because of Habib's faulty Arabic: if the leader's prayer is invalid, religious law dictates that it renders invalid the prayer of all those whom he leads. So, contrary to recommended practice, Hasan decided to pray on his own. That same night he had a vision in which Allah reprimanded him for entertaining the idea that a few errors of pronunciation could cancel out the devotional fervour of Habib's prayer. (Lings, *What is Sufism?*, 105)

At times Sufi teachings have a mind-stopping simplicity and directness similar to the methods employed by the Zen masters. Superficial similarities of this kind are, however, of secondary importance. What counts is the unexpected 'pause' these methods impose on the incessant chatter that normally fills our minds. The resultant mental vacuum can be likened to a garden, freshly weeded and dug over, ready for sowing or planting. Such is the case of Hasan's encounter with a child carrying a light. When Hasan asked him where the light came from, the child blew it out and said: 'Now you tell me where it has gone.' (Idries Shah, *The Way of the Sufi*, 247)

The material world appeared ever more seductive in the light of the unprecedented opulence and secular power that followed the geographical expansion of Islam. Hasan spoke out against corruption in high places, and warned against worldly attraction thus: 'Beware of this world with all wariness; for it is like to a snake, smooth to the touch, but its venom is deadly. Turn away from whatever delights thee in it . . . put off from thee its cares . . . The more it pleases thee, do thou be wary of it . . . for its hopes are lies, its expectations false . . .' (Abu Nu'aim, Hilya II, 134–40 in Arberry, *Sufism*)

> 'He that knoweth God loveth Him, and he that knoweth the world abstaineth from it.'
> (Lings, *What is Sufism?*, 105–6)

Rabi'ah (Rabi'ah al-'Adawiyyah: *c.*717–801)

Rabi'ah is one of the most famous women saints of Islam and a prominent figure in the Sufi tradition. (The word 'saint' is our translation of the Arabic *wali* – plural *awliya* – from *waliyu-llah*, meaning 'friend of Allah'.) She was born into a very poor family and was sold into slavery on the death of her parents, although her master later freed her when he became aware of her spiritual station. Rabi'ah spent most if not all of her life in Basra, and became famous in her own lifetime for her piety and asceticism.

Such was her renown that Rabi'ah was visited by many other prominent Sufis of the time. Although often described as a contemporary of Hasan of Basra, she was only about eleven years old when he died. Nonetheless, he appears in many of the stories that have come down to us about her. He is even reported to have asked her whether she wished them to marry. Rabi'ah replied: 'The tie of marriage applies to those who have being. Here being has disappeared, for I have become naughted to self and exist only through Him. I belong wholly to Him . . . You must ask my hand of Him, not of me.' (Fariduddin Attar, *Muslim Saints and Mystics*, 46)

A lifelong celibate, her devotion and love for Allah was so great that Rabi'ah is credited with being one of the first Sufis to give ecstatic voice to the theme of Divine Love. One of the ways in which she expressed her love for Allah was through short poems, which are among the first love poems in Sufi literature.

> I love Thee in two ways: one selfishly,
>> the other a love that is worthy of Thee.
> It is selfish love when I spend all my time
>> thinking exclusively of Thee and no other.
> The other kind of love is when the veil
>> is raised by Thee, thus revealing Thyself to me.
> Neither way am I praiseworthy.
>> In both the praise is all Thine. (Author's version)

For Rabi'ah it was enough to love Allah for Himself alone, and not in the expectation of receiving any reward or benefit in return. This intense and unconditional love also found expression through her prayers:

> O Lord! whatever share of this world Thou hast allotted to me,
> bestow it on Thine enemies; and whatever share of the next world
> Thou hast allotted to me, bestow it on Thy friends. Thou art
> enough for me.
>
> O Lord! if I worship Thee in fear of Hell, burn me in Hell;
> and if I worship Thee in hope of Paradise, exclude me from
> Paradise;
> but if I worship Thee for Thine own sake, withhold not Thine
> everlasting beauty!
> (Nicholson, *The Mystics of Islam*, 115)

Many of the stories about Rabi'ah display the immediacy and uncompromising directness of response that is characteristic of Allah's most intimate friends (*awliya*). In these stories, few if any concessions are made for either the innocence or the ignorance of those who came to her for spiritual guidance. Instead of tiptoeing around the hypersensitivities (imagined or otherwise) of the one standing before her, she would cut through them to the underlying truth of the matter. When a man came to her for advice, boasting that he had not sinned for twenty years, Rabi'ah replied: 'Alas, my son, thine existence is a sin wherewith no other sin may be compared.' (Lings, *What is Sufism?*, 97) Martin Lings describes similar utterances as 'the highest truth . . . stripped of all its coverings to be shot naked like an arrow into the heart of the "traveller" . . . all possibilities of interpretation at lower level are excluded lest the drowning man should have straws to clutch at.' (*What is Sufism?*, 98) Our existence is one of the straws we clutch at, yet in giving us our sense of 'me' it also perpetuates the dualistic mind-set that characterizes our separation from Allah and the Divine Unity. This is why the man's existence was a 'sin'. By contrast, the expression 'non-existence' refers to the unitive state. The following stories also illustrate the directness of Rabi'ah.

Rabi'ah saw a man wearing a bandage round his head.
　'Why are you wearing that bandage?'
　'Because my head hurts.'
　'How old are you?'

'Thirty.'

'Has your life involved much pain and suffering?'

'No.'

'For thirty years you have enjoyed good health and yet you never once wrapped yourself in the bandage of gratefulness. But as soon as your head hurts you put on the bandage of complaint!' (Fariduddin Attar, *Muslim Saints and Mystics*, 46–7)

One of Basra's leading scholars visited Rabi'ah when she was ill. As he sat at her bedside vilifying the world, she turned to him and said:

> 'You must really love the world a lot. If you didn't, you wouldn't go on about it so much. But then people don't find fault with things until they've bought them. If you weren't so attached to the world you would have nothing to say about it, good or bad. The reason you keep on talking about it is because, as the saying goes, if you really love something you never stop talking about it.' (*Muslim Saints and Mystics*, 50–1)

A door or gateway is a universal symbol, common to many spiritual traditions. In some contexts 'opening the door' can be interpreted as alluding to the opening of the heart, or to our passage through the illusory barrier that appears to separate us from Reality. Salih of Qazwin taught his followers, 'Knock, and the door will be opened.'

When Rabi'ah heard this, she said to Salih, 'How can you say, "The door will be opened"? It has never been shut.'

Hasan saw Rabi'ah by the side of a lake. Laying his prayer-rug on the surface of the water, he called out:

'Rabi'ah, come! Let us pray together.'

'Hasan, when you show off your spiritual wares in the bazaar of this world, you should at least display things that are beyond the reach of your fellow humans.'

Throwing her own prayer-rug high into the air, she flew up and sat on it.

'Come up here, Hasan, where people can see us both!'

Hasan remained on the ground, saying nothing: such a display was beyond his station. Rabi'ah sought to console him: 'Hasan, what you did any fish can do, and what I did any fly can do. The real work isn't about performing party tricks like these. So, let's get on with the work we're here to do.' (Fariduddin Attar, *Muslim Saints and Mystics*, 45)

The preceding anecdote is a reminder that the Sufis attach little importance to the outer expression of their spiritual state. Nor are their actions motivated by the desire for reward or a need for external recognition. As Rabi'ah said: 'Conceal your good deeds as you conceal your evil deeds.' (Ibn Khallikan, I, 34, no. 230)

Rabi'ah was once asked, 'Where do you come from?'
'From the other world.'
'And where are you going?'
'To the other world.'
'Then what are you doing in this world?'
'I am making a game of it.'
(Fariduddin Attar, *Tadhkirat al-Awliya*, 62)

Ibrahim ibn Adham (d.782)

Variously described as a prince, king or sultan, Ibrahim ibn Adham was born in Balkh, in the province of Khorasan in eastern Persia. Following a profound spiritual experience, he renounced his kingdom and earthly possessions to lead the life of a wandering dervish. He is said to have travelled westward to Syria, working there as a gardener until his identity was discovered. While travelling in the desert he met a monk called Father Simeon, from whom he is reported to have learned gnosis (*mar'ifa*). We are also told that he moved to Mecca, where a group of Sufis gathered around him, and he earned his living as a carpenter. According to some accounts he was killed during a naval expedition against Byzantium.

Attention has often been drawn to the similarities between the life of

Ibrahim ibn Adham, his spiritual awakening and subsequent asceticism, and that of the Buddha: both began their lives as princes, but renounced their worldly kingdoms to go in search of inner enlightenment. The province of Khorasan lay astride the caravan route (the famous Silk Road) to and from China, at the meeting-point of Middle and Far Eastern cultures, and the city of Balkh had been a flourishing Buddhist centre in pre-Muslim times. The ruins of Buddhist monasteries were still visible there centuries after the arrival of Islam.

Many anecdotal stories about Ibrahim ibn Adham describe his conversion or awakening. Others tell of his constant striving for self-effacement, or his extreme humility. In their conclusion, these stories frequently portray him as falling short of his aim – at times he despairs of ever being humble enough – yet he is never discouraged. In fact, one story tells how Gabriel was instructed to write Ibrahim's name at the top of the scroll on which are written the names of the friends of Allah, 'for on this Path hope materializes out of despair'. (Fariduddin Attar, *Muslim Saints and Mystics*, 76)

One night Ibrahim ibn Adham was fast asleep in bed when he was awakened by the sound of heavy footsteps walking across the roof of his palace. Intrigued, he went to the window and called out, 'Who is there?'

'A friend,' replied a voice. 'I have lost a camel, and I'm looking for it on your roof.'

'You fool!' responded Ibrahim. 'When did anyone ever find a camel on a roof?'

'O ignorant one!' came the reply. 'When did anyone wearing silk pyjamas and sleeping in a bed of solid gold attain union with God?'

Ibrahim ibn Adham was seated on his throne in the Great Hall of his palace. Gathered around him were his ministers and slaves. Suddenly a fearsome figure strode into the hall, straight up to the throne.

'What do you want?' demanded Ibrahim ibn Adham.

'I have just arrived at this caravanserai [caravan inn],' replied the man.

'You must be mad,' shouted Ibrahim. 'This is not a caravanserai. It's my palace.'

'And who owned this palace before you did?' asked the man.

'My father.'

'And before him?'

'My grandfather.'

'And before him?'

'So-and-so.'

'And before him?'

'So-and-so's father.'

'And where are they all now?'

'They have gone,' replied Ibrahim. 'They are dead.'

'Then is this not a caravanserai, where people come and go?'

As soon as the stranger had said these words he vanished. Ibrahim realized he had received a visit from Khidr, the immortal guide of the Sufi. (*Muslim Saints and Mystics*, 64)

One day Ibrahim ibn Adham was out hunting alone when he saw a hare. As he spurred his horse to take chase, he heard a voice say, 'It was not for this that you were created; this is not what you were sent to do.' Ibrahim stopped, looked around him, and seeing nobody, cursed Satan. He spurred on his horse, only to hear the voice a second time, 'It was not for this that you were created; this is not what you were sent to do.' As before, he stopped, looked around him, and seeing nobody, cursed Satan. As he dug his spurs into his horse's flanks a third time, the voice spoke again, but this time the words came from the pommel of his saddle. At this Ibrahim dismounted and surrendered himself to Allah. On the way back to his palace he espied one of his shepherds with whom he changed clothes, giving him his gold-embroidered cloak and cap in exchange for a patched robe of felt, the garment worn by dervishes. The angels look down from on high, crying aloud, 'He has cast off the filthy rags of the world and donned the glorious robe of poverty.' (Abu Nu'aim, Hilya VII, 368, in Arberry, *Sufism*)

When Ibrahim ibn Adham was employed as a gardener he was given the task of looking after the orchard. One day the owner of the orchard asked for some sweet pomegranates, but when Ibrahim took them to him he complained that they were bitter. The owner sent him away to get some more, but this second dishful was also bitter.

'How long have you been working in my orchard?' shouted the owner, 'And you still don't know what a ripe pomegranate should taste like.'

Ibrahim replied, 'I am paid to look after your orchard not to eat pomegranates, so I have never sampled one.'

'Only Ibrahim ibn Adham could practise such self-denial,' said the owner. 'Is that who you are?'

When his identity had been discovered, Ibrahim ibn Adham left his employer and resumed his wanderings through the desert. (Fariduddin Attar, *Muslim Saints and Mystics*, 76)

When a follower asked Ibrahim ibn Adham to define service, he replied, 'The beginning of service is meditation and silence, save for the recollection (*dhikr*) of God.' (Abu Nu'aim, Hilya VIII, 17, in Arberry, *Sufism*)

Sahl told how he was taken ill while travelling with Ibrahim ibn Adham. Ibrahim sold all that he possessed and spent it on the sick man. When the invalid was recuperating he asked for a certain delicacy, and Ibrahim went straight off and sold his donkey so that he could buy the delicacy for him.

When Sahl had almost recovered and was ready to travel again, he asked, 'Where is the donkey?'

'I sold it,' replied Ibrahim.

'What am I going to ride on?' asked Sahl.

'My shoulders,' said Ibrahim, and he carried Sahl on his back for the rest of the journey. (Idries Shah, *The Way of the Sufi*, 200)

One day Ibrahim ibn Adham came across a beggar who was complaining about being poor. Ibrahim said to him, 'I imagine the reason you're complaining about your poverty is because you paid nothing for it.'

'What nonsense,' replied the beggar. 'How can you buy poverty?'

'You can if you wish,' said Ibrahim. 'It cost me the kingdom of Balkh, but

I think I got a bargain.'

Ibrahim ibn Adham recalled, 'I once bought a slave.'

'What is your name?' I asked him,

'What you call me,' he answered.

'What do you eat?'

'What you give me.'

'What do you wear?'

'What you clothe me with.'

'What do you do?'

'What you command.'

'What do you desire?'

'What has a servant to do with desire?' he replied.

At this Ibrahim broke down. 'Oh, what a miserable creature I am,' he said to himself. 'All my life I thought I was being a servant of God, but I never learned the meaning of the word "servant" until now.' (Fariduddin Attar, *Muslim Saints and Mystics*, 75)

Shaykh Muzaffer Ozak tells the story of how, after a lengthy absence during which he had endured much hardship and passed many of the tests set by his shaykh, Ibrahim ibn Adham decided to return to his spiritual master. The shaykh called his dervishes together and told them to prevent Ibrahim ibn Adham from entering the city. When Ibrahim arrived at the gates he was driven away by a shower of verbal and physical abuse from his brother dervishes. He tried to enter by another gate and received identical treatment. The same happened at other gates until, determined to see his shaykh, Ibrahim ibn Adham eventually forced his way through and arrived at the *khaneka*. As he entered, an over-enthusiastic young dervish hit Ibrahim so hard that he drew blood. Ibrahim turned to the dervish and said in a calm voice, 'Why are you treating me like this? Don't you know that I am a dervish, just like you? Or do you still think I am the King of Balkh?'

When the shaykh heard of this, he remarked, 'Ibrahim ibn Adham has not yet forgotten who he once was. The taste for power and kingship is still ingrained in his memory.' (Shaykh Muzaffer Ozak, *Love is the Wine*, 20–1)

Shaqiq of Balkh (d.810)

A pupil of Ibrahim ibn Adham, Shaqiq of Balkh had been a successful merchant until he abandoned this occupation and gave away all his possessions on his conversion to the ascetic life. Stories and anecdotes about him portray him as a living example of the state (*hal*) known as 'trust in Allah' (*tawakkul*). A man of considerable learning, that part of his teaching which has come down to us reveals 'the beginnings of a formal system of self-discipline' of the kind developed by Sufis in the ninth century. (Arberry, *Sufism*, 39) Shaqiq was martyred in the wars that followed the death of Harun al-Rashid in 808. Shaqiq outlines three things that we need to practise:

> The *first* is this, that with your mind and your tongue and your actions you declare God to be One; and that, having declared Him to be One, and having declared that none benefits you or harms you except Him, you devote all your actions to Him alone. If you act a single jot of your actions for the sake of another, your thought and speech are corrupt, since your motive in acting for another's sake must be hope or fear; and when you act from hope or fear of other than God, who is the lord and sustainer of all things, you have taken to yourself another god to honour and venerate.
>
> *Secondly*, that while you speak and act in the sincere belief that there is no God except Him, you should trust Him more than the world or money or uncle or father or mother or any one on the face of the earth.
>
> *Thirdly*, when you have established these two things, namely, sincere belief in the unity of God and trust in Him, it behoves you to be satisfied with Him and not to be angry on account of anything that vexes you. Beware of anger! Let your heart be with Him always, let it not be withdrawn from Him for a single moment. (Nicholson, *The Mystics of Islam*, 42–3)

Shaqiq once said to his followers, 'I put my trust in Allah and travelled through the desert with only a small coin in my pocket. I went on the pilgrimage to Mecca, and when I came back the coin was still with me.'

A young man stood up and asked, 'If you had money in your pocket how can you say that you put your trust in something higher?'

'There is nothing I can say,' replied Shaqiq. 'This young man is right. If you put your trust in the invisible world, even the smallest precaution is out of place.' (Fariduddin Attar, *Kitab Ilahi*)

When Shaqiq stopped in Baghdad on the way to Mecca, he was summoned by the Caliph, Harun al-Rashid, who sought his advice.

'Suppose you were in the desert, dying of thirst. Would you be willing to give half of your kingdom for a drink of water?'

'I would,' replied the Caliph.

'And suppose after you had drunk the water you were unable to pass it, and were in danger of dying. Would you be willing to give half of your kingdom to someone who could cure you?'

'I would,' answered the Caliph.

'Then why do you boast about the greatness of your kingdom when you would willingly exchange it for a drink of water that would go in one end of you and out the other?' (Fariduddin Attar, *Muslim Saints and Mystics*, 137)

Sufyan al-Thauri (715–778)

Born in Kufa in Mesopotamia, Sufyan studied under many learned men, and founded a school of jurisprudence *(fiqh)*. He lived a strictly ascetic life, but in 775 he clashed with the authorities and was forced to go into hiding in Mecca. He died three years later in Basra. (Fariduddin Attar, *Muslim Saints and Mystics*, 129) Several anecdotes remind us that he was a contemporary of Rabi'ah, and often sought her advice on spiritual matters.

> One day Sufyan asked Rabi'ah, 'What is the best thing by which the servant seeks nearness to God Most High?' She said, 'That God knows

that the servant loves nothing in this world or the next except God.'
(Ernst, tr. *Teachings of Sufism*, 183)

One day Sufyan was walking through the town with a young dervish when they passed in front of a rich man's house. The door to the courtyard was open, and the dervish stopped to look inside. Sufyan reprimanded him, 'If only people like you spent less time staring at their palaces, rich people would not indulge in such ostentation. By staring at them in this way you become an accomplice in the sin of this extravagance. (Fariduddin Attar, *Muslim Saints and Mystics,* 131)

The following anecdote about Sufyan's dream reminds us that Sufis are not attached to the outcome of their actions; nor do they do things for any kind of reward, for to do so would be to act out of self-interest.

One night Sufyan dreamt he met a Sufi who claimed to have been rewarded for his charitable actions. 'I was even given a reward for picking up a piece of orange-peel and preventing someone from slipping on it.'

'How fortunate you were,' said Sufyan to the Sufi, 'not to have been punished on each of the occasions you gained personal pleasure from performing a charitable act.' (Idries Shah, *The Way of the Sufi*, 179)

Dawud al-Ta'i (d.777/782)

Dawud al-Ta'i came from Kufa. According to Attar, he studied under Abu Hanifa, but after meeting Habib al-Ra'i he converted to the ascetic life and threw all his books into the Euphrates river. (Fariduddin Attar, *Muslim Saints and Mystics*, 139) A renowned ascetic, he is said to have owned nothing but a rush mat, a brick which he used as a pillow, and a leather water-receptacle which he used for drinking and washing. (Nicholson, *The Mystics of Islam*, 36)

> 'Fast from this world and make death thy breakfast and flee from men as thou wouldst flee from beasts of prey.'
> (Qshayri, *Risalah*)

In his *Conference of the Birds*, Attar relates that when Ta'i lay dying someone asked him, 'O Ta'i, you have seen the essence of things, how is it with you now?' He said, 'I can say nothing about my state. I have measured the wind all the days of my life, and now the end is come I shall be buried, and so, good night.' (Fariduddin Attar, *The Conference of the Birds*, 68)

Fudayl ibn Iyad (Abu 'Ali al-Fozail ibn 'Iyaz al-Talaqani: d.803)

Born in Khorasan, he is said to have earned his living as a highwayman between Merv and Baward, but after his conversion to Islam he went to Mecca and Kufa. He was held in high regard as an authority on the Traditions and earned the respect of the Abbasid ruler Harun al-Rashid.

Hujwiri relates the following account of Fudayl's conversion. One day a merchant who was about to set out from Merv was advised by his friends to take an armed escort to protect him from Fudayl. The merchant ignored their advice and hired a professional Qur'an reader instead. When they arrived at Fudayl's ambush the reader was reciting the verse: 'Is it not time that the hearts of true believers should humbly submit to the remembrance of Allah?' (Qur'an 57:16). Fudayl, who was a God-fearing man, repented immediately, and sought to make amends to all those he had robbed. (Hujwiri, *Kashf al-mahjub*, 97–8)

One day Fudayl gave a fatherly kiss to a four-year-old child who was sitting on his lap, and the child asked: 'Father, do you love me?'

'Yes,' replied Fudayl.

'Do you love God?' asked the child.

'Yes.'

'How many hearts do you have?'

'One.'

'But how can you love two with one heart?' asked the child.

Fudayl understood that this was not the child speaking, it was a divine rebuke. Fudayl responded by giving his heart wholly to God. (Nicholson, *The Mystics of Islam,* 109)

Sayyida Nafisah (760–824)

The great granddaughter of Imam Hasan, the son of Imam Ali, Sayyida Nafisah was born in Mecca, and raised in Medina. She married Ishaq, the son of Imam Ja'far al-Sadiq, founder of the Ja'fari school of law, and was one of the first of the family of the Prophet Muhammad (*ahl al-bayt*) to leave the Arabian Peninsula when she and her husband moved to Egypt, to what is now the outskirts of modern Cairo. She was renowned for her piety and asceticism, and for her knowledge of the Qur'an and the Traditions. She was also a contemporary of Imam Shafi'i, founder of the Shafi'i school of jurisprudence, who was one of many religious scholars to discuss spiritual matters with her. (Shaykh Fadhlalla Haeri, *The Elements of Sufism*, 96) He died in 820, and in his will he asked that she perform the funeral prayers for him. At his death his body was taken to Sayyida Nafisah's house, for her constant fasting had rendered her too weak to leave it. (Helminski, *Women of Sufism*, 57)

During her lifetime Sayyida Nafisah was famed throughout Egypt for her good works and mystical powers. She also dug her own grave in her house, and as an act of devotion sat in it and recited the Qur'an six thousand times. When she died her husband wanted to take her body back to Medina for burial, but the people begged him to let her be buried in the land where she had died, and so she was laid to rest in her house in the grave which she had dug many years earlier. The site is now occupied by her mausoleum and mosque, and to this day pilgrims come from afar to visit her shrine. (*The Elements of Sufism*, 95–6)

Fatima of Nishapur (d.838)

Fatima of Nishapur has been described as 'one of the greatest female gnostics'. She spent most of her time in Mecca, and also visited Jerusalem. She was held in very high regard by both Dhu 'l-Nun al-Mesri and Bayazid Bistami (*see below*). Bayazid said of her that she was the 'one true woman' he had encountered in his entire life. (Cornell, *Early Sufi Women*, 142, 144) He said of her: 'There was no station [on the Way] about which I told her that she had not already undergone.' (Nurbakhsh, *Sufi Women*, 162) Dhu 'l-Nun considered her to be his teacher, and one of the greatest Sufis of his time. She advised him: 'In all your actions, watch that you act with sincerity and in opposition to your lower self (*nafs*).' (*Sufi Women*)

Al-Muhasibi (Harith b. Asad al-Muhasibi: 781–857)

Born in Basra, al-Muhasibi moved at an early age to Baghdad, the recently-built Abbasid capital, where he spent most of his life. There he studied the Traditions, and became closely involved with the leading figures of the time. Al-Muhasibi was one of the first Sufis to attempt to reconcile the Law (*shari'ah*) and the Path (*tariqah*), (Danner, *The Islamic Tradition*, 93) and his many writings – in particular his *Kitab al-Ri'aya* – were to have a profound influence on the thought of later Sufis, such as al-Ghazali. Professor Arberry notes that the larger part of al-Muhasibi's writings are on the subject of self-discipline, and that his name is itself connected with the Arabic word for self-examination: *muhasaba*. (Arberry, *Sufism*, 47) In another work he describes al-Muhasibi as 'one of the greatest figures in the history of Islamic mysticism.' (Fariduddin Attar, *Muslim Saints and Mystics*, 143)

One of al-Muhasibi's most famous pupils was al-Junayd, who gives an interesting insight into the nature of the teacher-pupil relationship in general, and of his own relationship with his master in particular. Junayd relates that his master would call at his house and invite him out. When the two men arrived at a certain place, al-Muhasibi would sit down and say to his pupil, 'Ask me a question.' Junayd would respond, 'I don't have a question to ask you,' to which his master would say, 'Ask me whatever comes into your mind.' Questions would then flood into Junayd's mind, and he would address them to his master, who would provide an immediate response. Afterwards al-Muhasibi would return to his own home, where he would turn these question-and-answer sessions into books. (Abu Nu'aim, *Hilya* X, 54, in Arberry, *Sufism*)

The following lines from al-Muhasibi's treatise on Love (*fasl fi 'l-mahabba*), are part of his response to a question about Original Love: 'The clearest sign of the love of God is excessive pallor, associated with continuous meditation, and prolonged vigil accompanied by complete self-surrender, obediently and with great haste ere dread death come upon him; and the lover speaks of love according to the measure of the Light bestowed upon him. Hence it is said, that the sign of the love of God is the indwelling of God's Favours in the hearts of those whom God has singled out for His Love.' (*Hilya* X, 79, in Arberry, *Sufism*)

> Meditation is the chief possession of the gnostic.
> (Smith, *Readings from the Mystics of Islam,* 14)

Dhu 'l-Nun (Dhu 'l-Nun al-Mesri: c.796–861)

A contemporary of al-Muhasibi, Dhu 'l-Nun was born of Nubian descent at Akhmim in Upper Egypt. It is said that he could read Egyptian hieroglyphs and was familiar with ancient Hermetic wisdom (named after Hermes, the Greek name for the Egyptian god Thoth). He was also an alchemist. He studied under various teachers and left Egypt to travel extensively in Arabia and Syria. During his travels he met Fatima of Nishapur, a famous woman Sufi of Khorasan, from whom he sought spiritual and doctrinal advice. (Cornell, *Early Sufi Women*, 142) In 829 he was arrested for heresy and imprisoned in Baghdad, but was released and returned to Cairo, where he died. Dhu 'l-Nun is reputed to have been one of the first to discuss the Sufic spiritual 'states' (*ahwahl*) and 'stations' (*maqamat*) (*Early Sufi Women*, 142n) and, according to Professor Nicholson, 'above all others [he] gave to the Sufi doctrine its permanent shape.' (Arberry, *An Introduction to the History of Sufism*, 44)

> 'The Sufi is he whose language, when he speaks, is the reality of his state.'
> (Hujwiri, *Kashf al-Mahjub*, 36)

In his prayers Dhu 'l-Nun expresses the Sufis' recognition of the Divine Unity:

> O God, I never hearken to the voices of the beasts or the rustle of

the trees, the splashing of the waters or the song of the birds, the whistling of the wind or the rumble of thunder, but I sense in them a testimony to Thy Unity (wahdaniya), and a proof of Thy Incomparableness; that Thou art the All prevailing, the All-knowing, the All-wise, the All-just, the All-true, and that in Thee is neither overthrow nor ignorance nor folly nor injustice nor lying. O God, I acknowledge Thee in the proof of Thy handiwork and the evidence of Thy acts: grant me, O God, to seek Thy Satisfaction with my satisfaction, and the Delight of a Father in His child, remembering Thee in my love for Thee, with serene tranquillity and firm resolve.

(Abu Nu'aim, *Hilya* IX, 342, in Arberry, *Sufism*)

Dhu 'l-Nun's poetry recalls the passionate language of Rabi'ah in its expression of the spiritual relationship between lover and Beloved.

> I die, and yet not dies in me
> The ardour of my love for Thee,
> Nor hath Thy love, my only goal,
> Assuaged the fever of my soul.
>
> To Thee alone my spirit cries;
> In Thee my whole ambition lies,
> And still Thy Wealth is far above
> The poverty of my small love.
> (*Hilya* IX, 390, in Arberry, *Sufism*)

A young man was always speaking out against the Sufis. One day, Dhu 'l-Nun removed a ring from his finger and gave it to the young man, saying, 'Take this ring to the bazaar and see if any of the stallholders will give you a dinar for it.'

He did as instructed, but no one in the bazaar was prepared to offer him more than a meagre dirham for the ring.

When the young man brought the ring back, Dhu 'l-Nun said to him, 'Now, take it to a real jeweller and see what value they put on it.'

The jeweller priced the ring at a thousand dinars.

Astounded by the difference in value, the young man took the ring back to Dhu 'l-Nun, who said to him, 'You know as much about the Sufis as those stallholders in the bazaar know about jewellery. If you want to learn the value of jewellery, ask a jeweller.' (Fariduddin Attar, *Muslim Saints and Mystics*, 97)

> A hermit said to Dhu 'l-Nun, 'O my son, one who is intimate with God has received four gifts: an honour which need be known to none, a knowledge without study, a richness without money, a joyful company without companion.'
> (Yafi'i, *Rawdh*, 53)

> The sign that a gnostic is separated from the divine presence is that he ceases to do the *dhikr*.
> (Dermenghem, *Vies des Saints musulmans*)

> An intending disciple said to Dhu 'l-Nun: 'Above everything in this world I wish to enrol in the Path of Truth.'
> Dhu 'l-Nun told him: 'You can accompany our caravan only if you can first accept two things. One is that you will have to do things which you do not want to do. The other is that you will not be permitted to do things which you desire to do. It is "wanting" which stands between man and the Path of Truth.'
> (Idries Shah, *Thinkers of the East*, 145)

One day Dhu 'l-Nun was asked, 'What is the way to God?' 'There is a lesser way, and there is a greater way,' he explained. 'Which of the two do you want to follow? If you follow the lesser way, you need to abandon the world, give up the temptations of the flesh, and stop your sinful ways. If you want the greater way, abandon everything but God and empty your heart of all things.' (Fariduddin Attar, *Muslim Saints and Mystics*, 96)

Bayazid al-Bistami (Abu Yazid al-Bistami: d.875/7)

The grandson of a Zoroastrian, Bayazid al-Bistami was born in Bistam in north-eastern Persia, and he died there. Many of his recorded sayings, and the stories related about him, concern the Sufi path of spiritual evolution, notably the state of passing-away (*fana'*) in which the individual self becomes absorbed in the Divine Unity, and there is no longer any separation between personal consciousness and a higher or universal consciousness. For Bayazid, 'the end of knowledge is that man comes to the point where he was at the origin.' (Stoddart, *Sufism*, 83) When we arrive at this state 'we' no longer exist, for as Bayazid explains: 'Creatures are subject to changing "states", but the gnostic has no "state", because his vestiges are effaced and his essence annihilated by the essence of another, and his traces are lost in another's traces.' (Nicholson, *The Mystics of Islam*, 17)

Bayazid is widely acknowledged as the first of the so-called 'ecstatic', 'intoxicated', or 'drunken' Sufis, who were famous (even infamous) for their ecstatic utterances (*shathiyat*). Some of these sayings, which were spoken while in an ecstatic state, were considered by the religious authorities (*'ulama'*) to be blasphemous. He said that he tried to find his way to God by praying with the pious, and by fasting with those who practised self-mortification, but he got nowhere. In the end, he asked: 'O God, what is the way to Thee?' The reply was: 'Leave yourself behind, and come to Me.' (Dermenghem, *Vies des Saints musulmans*, 219–20)

The point he was really making is clarified in another of his sayings: 'Those who are most veiled [separated] from God are three: First is the ascetic who is veiled by his asceticism, second is the worshipper who is veiled by his devotion, and third is the scholar who is veiled by his knowledge.' (Helminski, *Women of Sufism*, 47)

A recurring theme of Bayazid's is the principle that our spiritual state (*hal*) is not of our making. It is something that descends from God, and yet 'we' (our ego-centred personality) may unwittingly claim the credit for it, as related by Bayazid when he was brought into the Presence of God.

'Bayazid, how did you come to Me?'
'By renouncing the world.'
'The world for Me is little more than a gnat's wing. How did a minor renunciation bring you into My Presence?'
'Forgive me! I came to Thee by abandoning myself.'

'Is My Presence not proof of My Promise?'

'Forgive me! I came to Thee by Thyself.'

'It is in this way that We receive thee.' (Dermenghem, *Vies des Saints musulmans*, 220)

For Bayazid, union with the Divine gave rise to ecstatic states, and on one occasion he famously proclaimed: 'Glory be to Me! How great is My Majesty!' For obvious reasons, such a declaration was considered by many – especially the religious authorities (*'ulama'*) – to be blasphemous, for they interpreted it to mean that Bayazid was claiming to be God. From the Sufi point of view, however, 'Bayazid' no longer existed. Having 'passed away' and merged with the Divine, he had become Its mouthpiece.

Using the metaphor of the mirror, Bayazid expresses the same principle in a slightly different way: 'For thirty years God Most High was my mirror, now I am my own mirror and that which I was I am no more, for "I" and "God" is a denial of the unity of God. Since I am no more, God Most High is His own mirror. Now I say that God is the mirror of myself, for with my tongue He speaks and I have passed away.' (Nicholson, *The Mystics of Islam*, 17)

Elsewhere, he makes it abundantly clear what it is that has to 'pass away': 'I and Thou signify duality, and duality is an illusion, for Unity alone is Truth (*al-Haqq*, God). When the ego is gone, then God is His own mirror in me.' (Stoddart, *Sufism*, 83)

Both Attar and Rumi relate that when Bayazid's ecstatic state had passed, his disciples reported to him what he had said. 'If I say such a thing again,' he replied, 'take up your knives and kill me.' His disciples followed his instructions, and the next time he went into ecstasy and uttered similar words they attacked him with their knives. In Attar's account, Bayazid's form expanded until it filled the entire building, and yet however hard his disciples struck at him their blows were ineffectual. After a while the form shrank, and the disciples saw Bayazid sitting quietly in the prayer-niche. When his disciples told him what had happened, he said: 'This is Bayazid whom you see now. That was not Bayazid.' (Fariduddin Attar, *Muslim Saints and Mystics*, 115)

According to Rumi's version, each time Bayazid's disciples stabbed at him their knives rebounded, and they ended up cutting themselves. Rumi comments that those who have passed away in God are selfless, and therefore there is no 'self' to harm. Their form has passed away, too, and they have become a mirror in which nothing is seen but the reflection of another. If we hit it, we hit ourselves. If we see ugliness in it, it is our own. If we see Jesus and Mary, it is ourselves. Selfless and without form, the one who has passed away is neither this nor that. They are a mirror in which all we see is an image of ourselves. (Rumi, *Mathnawi*, Book IV, 389–91)

Bayazid was one of the first to employ the imagery of the Prophet's Night Journey or Ascension (*mi'raj*) as a vehicle for relating his own spiritual experience of union with the Divine, and of the 'flight of the alone to the Alone' (Fariduddin Attar, *Muslim Saints and Mystics*, 4):

> I saw that my spirit was borne to the heavens. It looked at nothing and gave no heed, though Paradise and Hell were displayed to it, for it was freed of phenomena and veils. Then I became a bird, whose body was of Oneness and whose wings were of Everlastingness, and I continued to fly in the air of the Absolute, until I passed into the sphere of Purification, and gazed upon the field of Eternity and beheld there the tree of Oneness. I cried: 'O Lord, with my egoism I cannot attain to Thee, and I cannot escape from my selfhood. What am I to do?' God spake: 'O Abu Yazid, thou must win release from thy thou-ness by following my Beloved [Muhammad]. Smear thine eyes with the dust of his feet and follow him continually'.
>
> (Hujwiri, *Kashf al-mahjub*, 238)

When Bayazid was in Hamadhan he bought a quantity of cardamom seed, and before setting out for Bistam he put the remainder of the seed in his carpet bag. Having reached his destination, he took out the seed and found that it contained a number of ants. Commenting upon the fact that he had taken the poor creatures away from their home, he immediately set out to travel back to Hamadhan – a journey of several hundred miles. (Nicholson, *The Mystics of Islam*, 108–9)

> One day someone came to his door, Bayazid asked him, 'Who are you looking for?'

'I am looking for Bayazid,' replied a voice.

'You poor man,' said Bayazid. 'For thirty years I, too, have been looking for Bayazid, but I have not yet found him.'

When Bayazid was asked how old he was, he said he was only four years old.

'How can this be?' they asked.

'I have been veiled from God for seventy years,' he replied, 'but I have only seen Him during the last four years. The period during which one is veiled does not belong to one's life.'

In his *Tadhkirat al-Auliya*', Attar records Bayazid as saying: 'For thirty years I went in search of God, and when I opened my eyes at the end of this time, I discovered that it was really He who sought for me.'

> 'This thing we tell of can never be found by seeking, yet only seekers find it.'
>
> (Dermenghem, *Vies des Saints musulmans*, 220)

Sahl al-Tostari (Sahl ibn Abd Allah al Tostari: *c*.815–896)

As his name implies, Sahl was born in Tostar. He studied with Sufyan al-Thauri, and met Dhu 'l-Nun al-Mesri. In 874 he was obliged to seek refuge in Basra, where he died.

One day while attending a religious meeting, Sahl's body began to shake violently and uncontrollably. A dervish who was present turned to another, and asked, 'What is his state (*hal*)?'

Sahl turned to the dervish, 'This was not, as you might have assumed, a sign that I was being invested with certain powers. On the contrary, it was a sign of my weakness.'

'If that was a sign of weakness,' said another, 'what then is power?'

'Real power,' replied Sahl, 'is when something like that happens, and mind and body manifest nothing at all.' (Idries Shah, *The Way of the Sufi*, 200)

God is (only) known by the union of contraries attributed to Him. (Burckhardt, *Introduction aux Doctrines ésoteriques . . .*, 32)

According to Hujwiri, Sahl said, 'If any one shuts his eye to God for a single moment, he will never be rightly guided all his life long.' (Hujwiri, *Kashf al-Mahjub*, 56)

Ju-nayd (Abu'l Qasim al-Junayd: d.910)

Generations of Sufis have considered Junayd to be one of the greatest among them. (Lings, *What is Sufism?*, 107) He was born in Persia, the son of a glass merchant and nephew of Sari al-Saqati, a leading figure in Sufi circles in Baghdad where Junayd's family settled. There he became a pupil of al-Muhasibi, and studied Islamic Law according to the Shafi'i school of jurisprudence. He eventually became the chief judge in Baghdad at a time when the orthodox religious authorities were increasingly hostile towards the Sufis, especially those of the 'intoxicated' or 'ecstatic' school with their seemingly blasphemous utterances. This school is often linked with the name of Bayazid al-Bistami, one of its earliest exponents. Junayd, on the other hand, is often described as the greatest exponent of the 'sober' school of Sufism. He is said to have taught his close followers behind locked doors, (Shaykh Fadhlalla Haeri, *The Elements of Sufism*, 97) and to have admonished his most famous disciple, Abu Bakr al-Shibli, for speaking too freely – Junayd held that the mystical knowledge of the Sufis was not to be divulged to others. (Lings, *What is Sufism?*, 109, n23) Nonetheless, he held Bistami in high regard, saying of him: 'The rank of Abu Yazid amongst us is even as that of Gabriel amongst the Angels.' (Hujwiri, *Kashf al-Mahjub*, 106)

Perhaps the most famous of the ecstatic Sufis was Mansur al-Hallaj, who had studied with Junayd. According to Attar, Junayd counselled Hallaj to practise patience and solitude. He also predicted that Hallaj would stain the gibbet with his blood. In response, Hallaj told him that the day this happened,

Junayd would be wearing the robes of a scholar. Some years later Hallaj was charged with heresy for proclaiming publicly, '*Ana al-Haqq*!' ('I am the Truth' – that is, 'I am God'), and condemned to death. When the warrant for Hallaj's execution was drawn up, Junayd was wearing his Sufi robe and did not sign. However, the caliph insisted that he sign the warrant. So Junayd changed his Sufi robe for the gown and turban of an academic. On the warrant he wrote: 'According to the outer law, he is guilty. As for the inner reality, God alone knows.' (Fariduddin Attar, *Muslim Saints and Mystics*, 265)

The hostility of orthodox religious authorities towards those who follow a mystical path is not restricted to Junayd's time: it is a phenomenon that has occurred in all religious traditions at one time or another. Junayd touched on the underlying truth of the situation when he said: 'None attains to the Degree of Truth until a thousand honest people have testified that he is a heretic.' (Idries Shah, *The Way of the Sufi*, 268) Junayd is credited with having developed a 'theosophical doctrine which determined the whole course of orthodox mysticism in Islam'. (*Muslim Saints and Mystics*, 199) His starting point was the promise, repeated several times in the Qur'an, that everything returns to God. Much of his writing and teaching concerns itself with the Sufi principle of self-annihilation in God (*fana'*) and a return to our primordial state and the Source of our being, leading to a 'life in God' (*baqa'*):

Junayd defines Sufism (*tasawwuf*) as meaning that 'God should cause thee to die from thyself and live in Him.' (Qushairi, *Risala*, 126)

> '*Tawhid* (Divine Unity) is the return of man to his origin, so that he
> will be as he was before he came into being.'
> (Affifi, *The Mystical Philosophy of Muyhid Din-Ibnul' Arabi*, 138)

Junayd was asked about the nature of love. He answered: 'Some say it is a state of harmony, and some say that it is altruism, and some say that it is something else.' (Nicholson, *The Mystics of Islam*, 114) He also defined love as the qualities of the Beloved replacing the qualities of the lover. In other words: real love is the passing-away of the self.

Junayd was once asked: 'Who is a gnostic?' He replied: 'The one who is not bound by time.' (Shaykh Fadhlalla Haeri, *The Elements of Sufism*, 98) His meaning is clarified by another saying of his: 'Unification is the separation of the eternal from that which was originated in time.' (*Hujwiri, Kashf al-Mahjub*, 281)

> 'The saint (Sufi) hath no fear, because fear is the expectation of some future calamity or of the eventual loss of some object of desire, whereas the saint is the son of his time: he has no future that he should fear anything; and as he hath no fear so he hath no hope, since hope is the expectation either of gaining an object of desire or of being relieved from a misfortune, and this belongs to the future; nor does he grieve, because grief arises from the rigour of time, and how should he feel grief who is in the radiance of satisfaction (*rida*) and the garden of concord (*muwafaqat*)?'
> (*Kashf al-Mahjub*, 216)

Idries Shah relates a story that illustrates how Junayd taught through practical demonstration, living out the particular lesson he wished to impart.

One day a group of aspiring seekers came to Junayd. When they found him surrounded by every imaginable luxury they left and went instead to an ascetic whose sole possessions were a mat and a jug of water.

One of the seekers said to the ascetic: 'We much prefer your simple manner and humble surroundings to the opulent excesses of Junayd. From the luxury in which he lives it would seem that he has abandoned the Path.'

'My friends,' said the ascetic, 'like most people you are too easily influenced by outward appearances. Mark the lesson well. Junayd is surrounded by luxury because he is unaffected by luxury; and I am surrounded by simplicity because I am unaffected by simplicity.' (Idries Shah, *Thinkers of the East*, 144)

> One of Junayd's followers came to him with a purse containing five hundred gold pieces.
>   'Have you any more than this?' asked the Sufi.
>   'Yes. I have.'
>   'Do you desire more?'
>   'Yes, I do.'

'Then you must keep it, for you are more in need than I; for I have nothing and desire nothing. You have a great deal and still want more.'
(Idries Shah, *The Way of the Sufi*, 72)

One day a certain disciple of Junayd's felt such shame when he was disciplined over a small matter that he left the *zawiyah*. Some days later Junayd was walking through the market with a group of his followers when he spotted the disciple, who immediately ran off. Junayd left the group and went after him. When he realized that the shaykh was following him the disciple walked faster. Eventually he found himself in a cul-de-sac. With no way out, he turned his face to the wall in shame. When Junayd caught up with him, the disciple asked: 'What are you doing here, Master?'

Junayd replied: 'When a disciple is up against the wall, then a shaykh can be of service.' So saying, he took the disciple back to the *zawiyah*. (Fariduddin Attar, *Muslim Saints and Mystics*, 210)

Junayd's followers were jealous of a certain disciple who appeared to enjoy their master's favour. Junayd confronted them, and told them that this disciple was superior to them in both conduct and understanding. To prove it to them, he conducted a little test. Ordering twenty birds to be brought to him, Junayd said to his disciples: 'Each of you take one of these birds, take it to a place where you cannot be seen and kill it, and then bring it back to me.'

They all went away and returned after a short while with the dead birds. That is, all except the favoured disciple. His bird was still alive.

'Why did you not kill it?' asked Junayd.

'Because you told us to kill it in a place where we could not be seen, but wherever I went I could be seen by God.'

Junayd addressed the jealous disciples: 'Now, compare that understanding with your own.' (*Muslim Saints and Mystics*, 210)

'The colour of the water is the colour of the vessel containing it.'

Part One

Al-Hallaj (Husayn ibn Mansur al-Hallaj: 858–922)

His ecstatic utterances, his condemnation for heresy and subsequent execution and the debate surrounding his violent death have made Hallaj the most controversial of the classical Sufis. Born in the Persian province of Fars, the son of a wool- or cotton-carder (Arabic, *hallaj*), he began travelling at the age of sixteen and during his life spent time in Tostar, Baghdad, Basra, Khorasan, Transoxiana and India – he also made three pilgrimages to Mecca. He was a close follower of several prominent Sufis of the period, including Sahl al-Tostari and Junayd. A controversial figure even in his own time, he held the view that the Sufi should become engaged in improving society. While some Sufis agreed with him, others (including Junayd) disagreed. Above all else Hallaj sought union with the Beloved. Indeed, he prayed for it: 'Oh Lord, remove by thy self, my "it is I" which torments me.' (Witteveen, *Universal Sufism*, 7)

Hallaj's passionate love for the Beloved and union with the Beloved were the principal themes of his poetry:

> I am He whom I love, and He whom I love is I;
> We are two spirits dwelling in one body.
> If thou seest me, thou seest Him,
> And if thou seest Him, thou seest us both.
> (Nicholson, *The Mystics of Islam*, 151)

> In that glory is no 'I' or 'We' or 'Thou'.
> 'I', 'We', 'Thou', and 'He' are all one thing.
> (*The Mystics of Islam*, 152)

Through severe ascetic practices Hallaj rose to complete union with the Beloved, and in doing so formulated a paradox with far-reaching implications:

> Whoso testifyeth that God is One thereby setteth up another beside Him (namely his own individual self as testifier).
> (*Akhbar al-Hallaj*, no. 49)

Commenting on this paradox, Martin Lings observes: 'If God alone *is*, no testimony can be valid except His. It is hypocrisy to affirm the Oneness of Being from a point of view which is itself in contradiction with the truth . . . The witness must be, not the self, but the Self.' (Lings, *What is Sufism?*, 75)

> I saw my Lord with the Eye of the Heart.
> I said: 'Who art thou?'
> He answered: 'Thou'.
> (Lings, *What is Sufism?*, 49)

Hujwiri relates that when Hallaj was staying in Kufa he received a visit from Ibrahim Kawas. He asked his visitor what he had gained from forty years of Sufism.

'I have concentrated my efforts on the principle of trust in God (*tawakkul*).'

'You have wasted your life developing your spiritual nature,' replied Hallaj. 'What of annihilation in Unification (*al-fana' fi'l-tawhid*)?'

Hujwiri explains what Hallaj meant by this: if someone spends their life working on their spiritual nature, they will need another life to work on their material nature. In other words, they will have reached the end of this life before they find God. (*Kashf al-Mahjub*, 205)

Hallaj severed his links with the Sufis for a period of time during which he continued to travel, meeting masters from other spiritual traditions. At the end of this time he concluded:

> I have meditated on the different religions, endeavouring to understand them, and I have found that they stem from a single principle with numerous ramifications. Do not therefore ask a man to adopt a particular religion (rather than another), for this would separate him from the fundamental principle; it is this principle itself which must come to seek him; in it are all the heights and all the meanings elucidated; then he will understand them.
> (Divan: *Muqatta'at*, L)

When he put on the Sufi robe again he took to preaching in the streets and market places of Baghdad, acquiring a large following of devotees who, inspired by his words, sought social and political reform as well as change in their own lives. Eventually he fell foul of those in power, in particular the Vizier, who sought to have him executed. It so happened that the utterances of ecstatics such as Bayazid al-Bistami had attracted the unwanted attentions of the religious authorities to the Sufis. Junayd counselled Hallaj to exercise restraint in his public teaching, but he was too intoxicated with the love of God to heed the warning.

> Thy Spirit is mingled with my spirit even as wine is mingled with
> pure water.
> When anything touches Thee, it touches me. Lo, in every case
> Thou art I!
> (Nicholson, *The Mystics of Islam*, 151)

> Love is that you remain standing in front of your Beloved:
> When you are deprived of all your attributes,
> Then His attributes become your qualities.
> (Shaykh Fadhlalla Haeri, *The Elements of Sufism*, 98)

The attributes of the Beloved are also known as the Divine Names, which are given elsewhere in this book. One of these attributes is *al-Haqq* ('the Truth'), but as one of the Divine Names it is also another name for God. As far as the religious authorities were concerned, when Hallaj had said, *'ana 'l-Haqq'* ('I am the Truth', or 'I am God'), he had preached incarnationism and was therefore guilty of heresy. The Sufis who were his contemporaries were in three minds about him. Some rejected his preaching; others accepted it; while yet others suspended judgement. For some, he was not guilty of heresy but his punishment was warranted because he had revealed the secret of the supreme mystery to all and sundry. For others, he had uttered the words during a moment of spiritual ecstasy, imagining himself to be united with the Divine Essence when in reality he was united with one of the Divine Attributes (*al-Haqq*, the Truth). For yet others, Hallaj's words proclaimed that there is essentially no separation between God and His creatures, since the Divine Unity contains all being. (Nicholson, *The Mystics of Islam*, 152) In effect, when

Hallaj said 'I am the Truth', there was no 'Hallaj'. It was a phrase he repeated at his martyrdom.

> If ye do not recognise God, at least recognise His signs. I am that sign, I am the Creative Truth (*ana 'l-haqq*), because through the Truth I am truth eternally . . . Pharaoh was drowned in the sea, yet he did not recant, for he would not acknowledge anything between him and God. And I, though I am killed and crucified, and though my hands and feet are cut off – I do not recant.
> (Nicholson, *Idea of Personality*, 32)

His actual execution, which is described by Attar in both the *Mantiq Ut-tair* (Conference of the Birds) and the *Tadhkirat al-Auliya'* (Memorial of the Saints), was a prolonged and bloody affair, and gave rise to numerous legends.

After Hallaj's death his close followers fled to Khorasan, taking his ideas with them. There they were taken up by Abu Sa'id and the later Persian mystical poets. (Fariduddin Attar, *Conference of the Birds*, 13) The thirteenth-century Persian poet Shabistari made a verbal play on the meaning of the name 'Hallaj' (wool-carder) in a poem in his *Gulshan i Raz* ('Secret Rose Garden'). The 'bush' in the last line is a reference to the burning bush which spoke to Moses (Qur'an 20:10–14):

> . . . When you have carded self
> Like the wool-carder, you will raise a cry.
> Oh! take the cotton of illusion from your ears,
> And hearken to the call of the One, the Almighty.
>
> . . . Why tarry till the last day
> When now, in the valley of peace,
> The very bush will say to you, 'I am Allah'?
> (Shabistari, *The Secret Rose Garden*, 85)

Part One

Al-Shibli (Abu Bakr Dulaf ibn Jahdar al-Shibli: d. 946)

The son of an official at the court in Baghdad, Shibli served as a chamberlain before being promoted to governor of Demavend. While in Baghdad for an investiture, he experienced a spiritual conversion and became a follower of Junayd. He became notorious for his eccentric behaviour and was eventually committed to an asylum.

After his conversion Shibli went to Junayd, and said: 'I am told that you are an expert on the pearl of divine knowledge. Will you either give it to me, or sell it?'

'I cannot give it to you, because you will have gained it too cheaply. And I cannot sell it to you, for you do not have the wherewithal to pay for it. You have no idea of its value. Immerse yourself, like me, in this ocean, and if you wait patiently the pearl will be yours.'

'What do I do now?' asked Shibli.

'Go and sell sulphur,' replied Junayd.

When Shibli had been selling sulphur for a year, Junayd said: 'Selling sulphur has set you up in business and made you well known. Now go and beg for a year.'

Shibli begged in the streets of Baghdad for a whole year, but everyone ignored him. At the end of the year he went back to Junayd, who said: 'Now you see how you count for nothing in the eyes of others. Don't waste time thinking about them, nor hold them in undue regard. For some time you were Governor of Demavend. Go back there and ask for forgiveness from everyone you wronged.'

For four years Shibli went from house to house until he had settled accounts with everyone, except for one person whom he was unable to trace. When he returned to Baghdad, Junayd said: 'You still have some lingering pride. Go and beg in the streets for another year.'

Every day Shibli gave Junayd the money he had received from begging. Junayd gave the money to the poor, and Shibli went without food until the next morning. After he had spent a year begging in this way, Junayd accepted him as a disciple on condition that he undertook to be a servant to the other disciples.

At the end of another year, Junayd asked: 'How do you see yourself now?'

'I consider myself to be the least of God's creatures,' replied Shibli.

'Now,' said Junayd, 'your faith is complete.' (Nicholson, *The Mystics of Islam*, 34–5)

One of the greatest barriers to inner awakening is the ego. On one occasion Shibli and Junayd's close followers were gathered together when one of those present began to praise Shibli in front of the others. Junayd interrupted the speaker and started to enumerate Shibli's faults. Embarrassed, Shibli discreetly made his way to the door. Once he had left the gathering, Junayd explained: 'I protected him with the shield of insult from the poisonous barbs of flattery.' (Shaykh Fadhlalla Haeri, *The Elements of Sufism*, 38)

> Shibli said: 'The Sufi is he that sees nothing except God in the two worlds.'
> (Hujwiri, *Kashf al-Mahjub*, 39)

Someone asked Shibli who it was that had been his first guide on the Path. 'A dog,' he replied. 'I saw him standing by the water's edge, dying of thirst. Every time he approached the water to drink, he was frightened by his own reflection. Thinking it was another dog, he retreated. In the end, however, he was so thirsty that he jumped in the water. When he did, the "other dog" disappeared. The dog's "other self", which had been the obstacle between the dog and what he sought, was no longer a barrier in his path. Likewise, when I realized that it was what I thought of as "me" that was the obstacle in my path, it disappeared. That is how the Path was first opened for me . . . by a dog.' (Idries Shah, *The Way of the Sufi*, 185)

> One day Shibli saw a man weeping, and asked: 'Why are you shedding these tears?'
> 'O shaykh,' he replied, 'I had a friend whose beauty refreshed

my soul. But yesterday he died, and I died too, from sorrow.'

'Is that so?' said Shibli. 'Don't grieve over him. Find yourself another friend, one who will not die and give you cause to mourn. A friend from whom we are parted by death will only bring sorrow. If we love the world's transient forms, we pay for our love a hundred times over with the misery we endure.'

(Fariduddin Attar, *The Conference of the Birds*)

Shibli said 'I imagined the beauty of Layla behind her bridal veils, but when I saw Layla, her beauty had no veils, and her beauty was more wonderful than I had imagined, and I understood that the veils were my eyelids and the beauty behind the closed eyes, in my imagination, was insufficient.'

(Shaikh Badruddin of Simawna, *Inspirations on the Path of Blame*, 121)

Shibli said: 'To feel at one with God for a moment is better than all men's acts of worship from the beginning to the end of the world.'

(Nicholson, *The Mystics of Islam*, 116)

Several anecdotes about Shibli refer to the eccentric behaviour that was to lead eventually to his committal to an asylum. In one such anecdote we are told he was in the habit of keeping sugar up his sleeve, and that he would give some to every boy he met, saying: 'Say Allah!'

Later he filled his sleeve with coins, saying: 'I will fill with gold the mouth of every one who says Allah once.'

Next he drew his sword: 'I will cut off the head of every one who mentions the name of Allah!'

'You used to give away sugar and gold. Why do you now want to cut our heads off?'

'At first I assumed people pronounced His name with knowledge and understanding,' explained Shibli. 'Now I know it was by rote and solely from habit. I cannot allow His name to be uttered in this way.'

After this Shibli wrote up the name of Allah on every available place. Then suddenly he heard a voice speaking to him: 'How much longer will you concern yourself with the name? If you are a true seeker, seek the Named!' (Faruddin Attar, *Muslim Saints and Mystics*, 279–80)

Hujwiri relates that one day when Shibli was in the bazaar people called out: 'This man is mad!' Shibli answered back: 'You think I am mad, and I think you are sane. May God increase my madness and your sanity!'

Hujwiri explains that Shibli's 'madness' was due to his intense love of God, whereas the people's 'sense' was due to their ignorance. In his answer Shibli was effectively saying: 'May God increase my madness so that I come closer to Him, and may he increase your sanity so that you distance yourselves ever further from Him.' (*Kashf al-Mahjub*, 156)

Abu Sa'id (Abu Sa'id ibn Abi 'l-Khayr: 978–1061)

Born in Mayhana, a city in the province of Khorasan, Abu Sa'id studied under a number of Sufi teachers, including Abu 'l-Fadl Hasan of Sarakhs. He popularized the use of poetry, especially the newly-invented *ruba'i* (quatrain), as a medium for expressing mystical ideas and spiritual states, either in public recitation or in teaching his followers. He also contributed to the establishment of the Sufi centre (Arabic: *zawiyah*; Persian: *khanaqah*; Turkish: *tekke*) as a place for spiritual training, and developed a code of conduct for dervishes. (Bayat & Jamnia, *Tales From the Land of the Sufis*, 29–30)

As has already been mentioned, the tenth and eleventh centuries were a time of considerable friction between the exoteric and esoteric aspects of Islam – that is, between orthodox Muslims and the Sufis – and Abu Sa'id was the subject of more than one assassination plot by zealous exotericists. The following *ruba'i*, in which he speaks for the Calendars or 'wandering dervishes', has been described as an 'open declaration of war against the Mohammedan religion'. (Nicholson, *The Mystics of Islam*, 90) In reality it may be more to do with the removal of every thing that stands between ourselves and God, even the externals of religion.

> Not until every mosque beneath the sun
> Lies ruined, will our holy work be done;
> And never will true Musulman appear
> Till faith and infidelity are one.
> (*The Mystics of Islam*, 91)

The last two lines convey the idea that no one can call themselves a true Muslim – that is, one who truly surrenders their individual self to God – until they have transcended the dualistic mind-set which perceives the world in terms of opposites, such as faith and infidelity. That Abu Sa'id's *ruba'i* is referring to the dualistic religious mind-set, which is characterized by talk of 'God' and 'other than God', rather than to religion *per se* becomes apparent when he makes a similar comment about Sufism.

> Abu Sa'id said, 'Even this Sufism is polytheism (*shirk*).'
> 'Why, O Shaykh?' they asked.
> He answered, 'Because Sufism consists in guarding the soul from what is other than God; and there is nothing other than God.'
> (Nicholson, *Studies in Islamic Mysticism*, 49-50)

Abu Sa'id said that to be a Sufi is to stop worrying, and the greatest cause of worry for us is our self. The more we worry about ourselves, the further we distance ourselves from God. (Smith, *Readings from the Mystics of Islam*, no. 50) He made the same point more succinctly when he said:

> Take one step out of thyself, that thou mayst arrive at God.
> (Nicholson, *Studies in Islamic Mysticism*, 50)

Ansari ('Abdallah al-Ansari: d.1088/9)

Born near Herat in Khorasan, Ansari was an eminent lawyer in the Hanbali school of jurisprudence. He wrote devotional works in Persian and Arabic and also works on the Sufis and on Sufi theory. Ansari and his older contemporary Abu Sa'id are considered to have laid the foundations for Persian Sufi poetry and its flowering in the writings of Sana'i, Attar, Rumi, and others. (Arberry, *Sufism*, 71–3)

The examples of Ansari's work given here contain several Sufi themes that bear repetition: humility; ignorance, or the lack of real knowledge; the Sufis' disinterest in party tricks; and the passing-away (*fana'*) of the ego-centred self.

> Would you be a pilgrim on the road of Love?
> The first condition is that you make yourself humble as dust and ashes.
> (Huxley, *The Perennial Philosophy*, 119)

> Men are like addicts of drink,
> Unaware of their own state.
> The wise are wide awake,
> Having cast out the spell.
> (Singh tr., *The Persian Mystics*, 53)

> If thou canst walk on water
> Thou art no better than a straw.
> If thou canst fly in the air
> Thou art no better than a fly.
> Conquer thy heart
> That thou mayest become somebody.
> (*The Persian Mystics*, 36)

> Know that when you learn to lose yourself, you will reach the Beloved. There is no other secret to be learnt, and more than this is not known to me.
> (Huxley, *The Perennial Philosophy*, 350)

Ghazali (Abu Hamid Muhammad al-Ghazali: 1058–1111)

Ghazali was born in Tus, in the province of Khorasan in northeast Persia. As a young man, he studied traditional Islamic theology (*kalam*) for several years. When he was thirty-three, the Seljuk vizier Nizam al-Mulk, founder of the Nizamiya Madrasa university in Baghdad, the Seljuk capital, appointed him professor of theology. Four years later, in 1095, he experienced a profound spiritual crisis and resigned from his teaching position. For the next twelve years he led the solitary life of an itinerant ascetic. During his travels he encountered many Sufis and eventually became one himself. He later returned to Tus, his birthplace, where he resumed teaching until his death.

The unfolding of Ghazali's own life – a knowledge of the outer law and an awakening to inner reality – in some ways parallels the traditional Sufi path. The integration of outer law and inner reality formed the basis of Ghazali's teaching when he returned from his years as a wanderer and he became one of the most influential of Islamic theologians. Following a period in which many Sufis had been persecuted by orthodox religionists, he was instrumental in establishing a more permanently harmonious and dynamic relationship between the outer and inner aspects of Islam.

Ghazali's years of spiritual search not only brought about his inner awakening and transformation but they were also the inspiration for a number of written works, including: *al-Munqidh min ad-Dalal* (*What Delivers from Error*), an analytical account of his spiritual development; *Bidayat al-Hidayah* (*The Beginning of Guidance*), which sets out religious practices and a code of conduct for 'seekers of knowledge'; *Tahafut al-Falasifa* (*The Incoherence of the Philosophers*), an attack on philosophy which provoked a response from the great philosopher Avicenna in his *Tahafut al-Tahafut* (*The Incoherence of the Incoherence*); and *Al-Maqsad al-asna fi sharh asma Allah al-husna* (*The Ninety-Nine Beautiful Names of God*).

Ghazali's greatest work is considered to be his *Ihya' 'Ulum al-Din* (*Revival of the Religious Sciences*), the title of which sums up his achievement for he revitalized Islam at a time when its inner reality was under threat from an over-concern with outer form. As he said: 'Those which are learned about, for example, the laws of divorce, can tell you nothing about the simpler aspects of spiritual life, such as the meaning of sincerity towards God or trust in Him.' The book was burned in public prior to the recognition of Ghazali as the greatest religious authority of his time. He not only shaped the development of Islam but it seems certain that he also exerted a considerable influence on Western thought and Christian philosophers of the Middle Ages.

Ahmad al-Ghazali (d.1123), Imam Ghazali's lesser-known brother, was also a Sufi. His writings on the theme of Love, Lover, and Beloved were to influence later generations of Sufis, including the Persian poet Jami.

In *The Way of the Sufi*, Idries Shah draws attention to an important aspect of Ghazali's work, saying: 'Eight hundred years before Pavlov, he pointed out and hammered home (often in engaging parables, sometimes in startlingly "modern" words) the problem of conditioning.' He continues: '. . . the ordinary student of things of the mind is unaware of the power of indoctrination. Indoctrination, in totalitarian societies, is something which is desirable providing it furthers the beliefs of such societies. In other groupings its presence is scarcely even suspected. This is what makes almost anyone vulnerable.' In a footnote he comments that in spite of all the scientific evidence to the contrary, we find it hard to accept that our beliefs are not always linked to our intelligence, our culture, or our moral values. We are therefore 'almost unreasonably prone to indoctrination'. (Idries Shah, *The Way of the Sufi*, 55)

Idries Shah was writing in the late 1960s. Pavlov and the techniques of conditioning and indoctrination are less topical in the first decade of the twenty-first century. But this does not mean that they have gone away. If anything, they are employed with much greater subtlety and on a much bigger scale, thanks to our exposure to wall-to-wall media. And yet, at the same time, we probably believe that we have greater freedom of thought than ever before. This makes Ghazali's observations about discovering our original nature (*fitrah*) and looking for 'knowledge of what things really are', particularly relevant today.

> To thirst after a comprehension of things as they really are was my habit and custom from a very early age. It was instinctive with me, a part of my God-given nature, a matter of temperament and not of my choice or contriving. Consequently as I drew near the age of adolescence the bonds of mere authority (*taqlid*) ceased to hold

me and inherited beliefs lost their grip upon me, for I saw that Christian youths always grew up to be Christians, Jewish youths to be Jews and Muslim youths to be Muslims. I heard, too, the Tradition [*ḥadith*] related from the Prophet of God according to which he said: 'Everyone who is born is born with a sound nature; it is his parents who make him a Jew, a Christian or a Magian [Zoroastrian]'. My inmost being was moved to discover what this original nature [*fitrah*] really was and what the beliefs derived from the authority of parents and teachers really were, and also to make the distinctions among the authority-based opinions, for their bases are oral communications and in distinguishing between the true and the false in them, there are differences of view.

I therefore said within myself: 'To begin with, what I am looking for is knowledge of what things really are, so I must undoubtedly try to find what knowledge really is'.

(*The Faith and Practice of Al-Ghazali*, 19)

In the light of what Ghazali has to say about conditioned beliefs, it would seem that this was the underlying cause of his spiritual crisis. That is, a conflict between what he had been taught and what he knew in his spiritual heart. Ghazali's biographical writings describe his spiritual crisis in detail, with him being pulled first one way by 'the voice of religion' (the inner voice) and then the other by 'the Tempter' (his own mental chatter). In addition to these mental arguments, it is worth noting that the physical symptoms he manifested at the time were also recognized as being caused by his spiritual crisis – knowledge of the body-mind-spirit relationship is nothing new:

One day I decided to leave Baghdad and to give up everything; the next day I gave up my resolution. I advanced one step and immediately relapsed. In the morning I was sincerely resolved only to occupy myself with the future life; in the evening a crowd of carnal thoughts assailed and dispersed my resolutions. On the one side the world kept me bound to my post in the chains of covetousness, on the other side the voice of religion cried to me, 'Up! Up!' Thy life is nearing its end, and thou hast a long journey to make. All the pretended knowledge is nought but falsehood and fantasy. If thou dost not think now of thy salvation, when wilt thou think of it? If thou dost not break thy chains today, when wilt thou break them? Then my resolve was strengthened; I wished to give up all and flee; but the Tempter, returning to the attack, said, 'You are suffering from a transitory feeling, don't give way to it, for it will soon pass. If you obey it, if you give up this fine position, this honourable post exempt from trouble and rivalry, this seat of authority safe from attack, you will regret it later on without being able to recover it.'

Thus I remained torn asunder by the opposite forces of earthly passions and religious aspirations, for about six months from the month of Rajah . . . [in 1095]. At the close of them I yielded and gave myself up to destiny. God caused an impediment to chain my tongue and prevented me from lecturing. Vainly I desired, in the interest of my pupils, to go on with my teaching, but my mouth became dumb. The silence to which I was condemned cast me into a violent despair; my stomach became weak, I lost all appetite; I could neither swallow a morsel of bread nor drink a drop of water.

The enfeeblement of my physical powers was such that the doctors, despairing of saving me, said, 'The mischief is in the heart, and has communicated itself to the whole organism; there is no hope unless the cause of his grievous sadness be arrested.
(Ghazali, *The Confession of Al-Ghazzali*, 11. Quoted in Arasteh, *Growth to Selfhood*, 42–43)

Having studied with the theologians, the philosophers and 'authoritative instruction', Ghazali turned to the mystics, or Sufis. He knew that the 'way' of the mystics included 'both intellectual belief and practical activity', of which the latter 'consists in getting rid of the obstacles in the self and in stripping off its base characteristics and vicious morals, so that the heart may attain freedom from what is not God . . .' He continues:

It became clear to me . . . that what is most distinctive of mysticism is something which cannot be apprehended by study, but only by immediate experience (*dhawq* – literally 'tasting'), by ecstasy and by a moral change. What a difference there is between *knowing* the definition of health and satiety, together with their causes and presuppositions, and *being* healthy and satisfied! . . . Similarly there is a difference between knowing the true nature and causes and conditions of the ascetic life and actually leading such a life and forsaking the world.

I apprehended clearly that the mystics were men who had real experiences, not men of words, and that I had already progressed as far as was possible by way of intellectual apprehension. What remained for me was not to be attained by oral instruction and study but only by immediate experience and by walking in the mystic way.

(*The Faith and Practice of Al-Ghazali*, 57, 58)

When Ghazali eventually left Baghdad he is said to have taken two mules with him, loaded with books. On the road he was held up by a robber who demanded that Ghazali hand the books over to him. The scholar refused, offering him everything but the books. But the robber insisted, and made off with them. Some years later, after he had met the Sufis and experienced his inner awakening, he was in Mecca when Khidr appeared to him. The immortal guide informed him that if the books had not been taken from him, Ghazali would have remained enslaved by them. Had this been the case he would not have awakened to the real 'Book' of knowledge within his heart. (Shaykh Fadhlalla Haeri, *The Elements of Sufism*, 39)

Asked what he had learned from the Sufis, Ghazali replied: 'Two things. One is that time is like a sword, if you don't cut through it, it will cut you down. The second thing I've learned is that if you do not put yourself to work for the good, it will preoccupy you with evil'.

Like many Sufis, Ghazali was skilled in the science of the psyche. His solution to clearing the human mind of its accumulated rubbish was simple:

If we would like to clean the well of the psyche of the polluted rubbish which constantly flows into it by the social currents, we must first stop the flow of such polluted matter and then find a good cleaning detergent and clean the well. Then we must let clean water flow in.

(Ghazali, *The Alchemy of Happiness*, 14. Quoted in Arasteh, *Growth to Selfhood*, 16)

Ghazali's 'period of retirement' lasted 11 years, until 1106. He was reluctant to go back to teaching, because, as he said: 'To go back is to return to the previous state of things.' But he was also aware of the profound change that had taken place within him: 'Previously, however, I had been disseminating the knowledge by which worldly success is attained; by word and deed I had called men to it; and that had been my aim and intention. But now I am calling men to the knowledge whereby worldly success is given up and its low position in the scale of real worth is recognized.'

He continued with his teaching for the remainder of his life. During what was to be his final illness he wrote a poem which was found beneath his head after his death. It included the following lines:

> Say to my brethren when they see me dead,
> and weep for me, lamenting me in sadness:
> 'Think ye I am this corpse ye are to bury?
> I swear by God, this dead one is not I.
> When I had formal shape, then this, my body,
> Served as my garment. I wore it for a while . . .
>
> A bird I am: this body was my cage
> But I have flown leaving it as a token.'
> (Tr. Martin Lings.)

Imam Ghazali and the reinstatement of the *tariqah* at the heart of Islam bring to a close the period during which the religious authorities had shown open hostility towards the Sufis. The end of one period heralded the dawn of another: the 'Golden Age' of the twelfth and thirteenth centuries. The need for the Sufis to produce textbooks and treatises to placate the religious authorities had passed. A change of style and content is already apparent in the writings of Imam Ghazali and so it seems appropriate to change our own style of presentation. In the next section we take a longer look at the writings of Attar, Ibn 'Arabi, Rumi and Shabistari.

Part Two

Chapter Seven:

The Writings of the Sufis

Fariduddin Attar and
The Conference of the Birds

*O Thou who art not seen although Thou makest us to know Thee,
everyone is Thou and no other than Thou is manifested. The soul is
hidden in the body, and Thou art hidden in the soul. O Thou who art
hidden in that which is hidden, Thou art more than all. All see
themselves in Thee and they see Thee in everything.*
(Fariduddin Attar, *The Conference of the Birds*, tr. C. S. Nott, 4)

Little is known for certain about the life of Fariduddin Attar, except that he was
born near Nishapur in northeast Persia during the second quarter of the
twelfth century and he became one of the first great Persian Sufi poets. He is
said to have been educated at a theological school, and at some stage he
acquired a pharmacy, or possibly a perfumery business, in Nishapur, where it
is said that he employed some thirty people. The name 'Attar' translates as
'chemist' or 'perfume seller' and has its roots in the word from which we get
'attar', as in 'attar (essential oil) of roses'.

   Tradition has it that Attar's inner life began in earnest after a chance
conversation with a dervish while working in his pharmacy. Accounts differ as

to what precisely occurred, but this should not be taken to mean that one particular account is right and the others wrong. Anecdotal stories from the lives of the Sufis are usually more concerned with expounding Sufi teaching and the knowledge of the inner life than with historical accuracy, and so it is up to us whether we understand them in a literal or allegorical sense. For instance, Idries Shah suggests that the story told about Attar's conversion is used by the Sufis 'to illustrate the need for balance between material and metaphysical things'. (Idries Shah, *The Sufis*, 118)

One day a wandering dervish came to the door of Attar's pharmacy and gazed in open-mouthed wonder at the variety of merchandise and the owner's evident wealth. Then with tears in his eyes he looked hard at Attar. The chemist asked him what he was staring at.

'I was wondering how you are going to die,' answered the dervish.

'I will die the same as you,' said the chemist.

'No, you won't', said the dervish. 'Dying is easy for me. All I have in the world is this cloak. But you, how are you going to die when you have to leave all your wealth and possessions behind?' And with that the dervish lay down on the ground and died.

With its echoes of the *hadith* 'Die before you die', the incident was a profound awakening for Attar. He closed his business and entered a Sufi community under Shaykh Ruknuddin. On leaving the community he travelled to Egypt, Damascus, Mecca, Turkestan and India. He also began to write poetry and gather material for his prose work, *Tadhkirat al-Auliya* (Memorial of the Saints), a collection of biographies and anecdotal stories about the Sufis, who are also known as the 'Friends of God' (*al-Auliya*). Attar was possibly tried for heresy and banished from Nishapur late in life, although he had returned there by the time he died. As with the account of his spiritual awakening, the story of how he met his death has several variations.

It is said that Attar was taken prisoner by a Mongol when Genghis Khan's hordes invaded Persia. His captor was offered a thousand pieces of silver for him, but the Sufi advised him to hold out until such time as he was offered a better price. The Mongol followed his advice and refused to sell him. Later on, the Mongol was offered a sack of straw in exchange for his prisoner. 'Take the straw,' said Attar, 'for that is all I am worth.' In a fit of rage the Mongol killed him.

There is some debate about the year in which Attar died, which throws the precise circumstances of his death into question. If he was born in 1120, as some authorities suggest, he would have been well over a hundred years old at the time of the Mongol sack of Nishapur in 1229. However, other authorities suggest that he died in around 1220. Whichever is true, the way in which Attar died offers a dramatic illustration of the lower and higher selves in action. The Mongol, a man of greed and violence, embodies the lower self, whereas Attar, the man of humility and wisdom, represents the higher self.

The Writings of Attar

Attar is reputed to have written well over a hundred books of which only some thirty have survived, but it is not certain how many of the works attributed to him were authentically his. Persia already had an established tradition of Sufi poetry, written by such figures as Omar Khayyam, famous for his *Rubaiyat* (a collection of quatrains, or *ruba'i*), who was, like Attar, a native of Nishapur. Another important contributor to the tradition was Hakim Sana'i, whose use of the *mathnawi* (rhyming couplet) in his *Hadiqat al-haqiqa* ('Garden of the Truth'), as a vehicle for Sufi teaching established a model that was to be followed by Attar – and later by Rumi, in his own *Mathnawi*.

The Book of God and The Book of Secrets
Two important books in which Attar used the *mathnawi* form are the *Book of God* or *Divine Book* (*Ilahi-nama*), a book of Sufi instruction, and the *Book of Secrets* (*Asrar-nama*). The latter is a collection of short stories illustrating Sufi principles, a copy of which he gave to Jalaluddin Rumi who, as a young boy, visited Attar in Nishapur when his family were fleeing from the approaching armies of Genghis Khan. Attar was already an old man at the time of their meeting and the two never met again. Yet Rumi, who is the better known of the two in the modern West, acknowledged his indebtedness to Attar: 'All I have said about the Truth, I have learned from Attar.' (Mojdeh Bayat and Mohammad Ali Jamnia, *Tales from the Land of the Sufis*, 48. The authors include the story of Bahlul from the *Ilahi-nama* in their book and list the following English translation in their bibliography: *The Ilahi-nama or Book of God*, tr. J. A. Boyle, Manchester University Press, 1976.)

The Memorial of the Saints

Attar's one surviving work in prose, the *Memorial of the Saints* (*Tadhkirat al-auliya*), is a compilation of anecdotal stories, parables, miracles and biographical details about the Muslim saints, or 'Friends of God' (*al-auliya*) as the Sufis are sometimes known. Attar collected the material for his book during his travels, and also drew on the work of earlier biographers (or 'hagiographers', a term often used to refer to those who write the lives of saints). The *Memorial of the Saints* covers a period of 200 years from Imam Ja'far al-Sadiq (*c.*700–765), the Sixth Imam, to the death of Hallaj (858–c.922), although some manuscripts contain a supplement which continues beyond this date. Professor A. J. Arberry extends his selected translation to include Shibli (d.946), whose death 'marks the end of the formative period of Sufism'. (Fariduddin Attar, *Muslim Saints and Mystics*, tr. A. J. Arberry, 17)

Anecdotal stories told about the Sufis from Attar's *Memorial* have been retold many times across the centuries; their shape, and even the name of the central character, has changed along the way. The accounts of the lives of the Sufis (up to and including Shibli) within the pages of this book owe much to Attar's *Memorial* (as well as to one of Attar's own sources, the *Kashf al-Mahjub*, by Hujwiri), and so only a couple of short extracts are given here. They are both 'miracle stories' involving Ibrahim ibn Adham, Prince of Balkh who, like the Buddha, gave up his kingdom to lead the humble life of a wandering ascetic.

> Ibrahim ibn Adham wished to make a journey by sea, but the fare was one dinar and he had no money.
>
> He prayed two *rak'as* (cycles of the ritual prayer), and said, 'O Lord, they are asking me for money and I have none.'
>
> The whole sea was immediately turned to gold. Ibrahim gathered up a handful and gave it to the man collecting the fares.

> Ibrahim ibn Adham was sitting on the bank of the river Tigris, sewing a patch on his threadbare robe. A passer-by recognized him, and asked: 'You gave up such a great kingdom. What did you get in return?'
>
> As Ibrahim ibn Adham turned to answer, his needle dropped

into the river. Pointing at the spot where it had fallen in, he said loudly: 'Give me back my needle!'

A moment later a thousand fish stuck their heads out of the water, each holding a gold needle in its mouth.

'No. I want my own needle,' said Ibrahim.

An insignificant little fish held up Ibrahim's needle in its mouth.

Taking his needle from the fish, Ibrahim turned to the passer-by, and said: 'This is the least I got from abandoning my kingdom. The rest is not for you to know.'

(Adapted from Fariduddin Attar, _Muslim Saints and Mystics_, tr. A. J. Arberry, 78)

The Conference of the Birds

Written in the _mathnawi_ form and comprising some 5,000 couplets, Attar's best-known work is a timeless poetic allegorization of the quest for union with God. In essence the storyline is very simple: the bird kingdom awakens to the fact that it is the only kingdom on earth to have no king, and so the birds decide to find one. The hoopoe, who is elected to be their guide, tells them that they already have a mysterious king who goes by the name of 'Simurgh'. He lives at the farthest ends of the world, beyond the mountains of Kaf, and to reach him they have to pass through seven valleys.

At first the birds are eager to set off on their quest, but when they hear that the journey will be perilous some of them have second thoughts and make excuses not to go. The hoopoe listens to the reservations of each bird in turn, either answering their queries directly or wrapping the answer in a story. When the birds set off it is not long before they run into difficulties and their will weakens. To encourage them to continue with their journey the hoopoe describes what they will encounter in each of the valleys, illustrating the description with stories. In the end only thirty birds out of the entire bird kingdom reach the Simurgh's palace. At first they are refused entry, even told to retrace their steps, but this is simply to test their resolve to complete their journey. They pass the test and enter into the presence of the Simurgh.

The birds' meeting with the Simurgh requires some additional explanation. In Persian, the word _si_ means 'thirty' and _murgh_ means 'bird(s)'. So when the _thirty birds_ who complete the journey reach their goal and enter

into the presence of the *Simurgh*, they find that the Simurgh is themselves
and they are the Simurgh:

> There in the Simurgh's radiant face they saw
> Themselves, the Simurgh of the world – with awe
> They gazed, and dared at last to comprehend
> They were the Simurgh and the journey's end.
> They see the Simurgh – at themselves they stare,
> And see a second Simurgh standing there;
> They look at both and see the two are one . . .
> (Fariduddin Attar, *The Conference of the Birds*,
> tr. Afkham Darbandi and Dick Davis, 219)

The end of duality signifies the birds' annihilation in the Divine Unity and the
completion of their journey. Another element to consider is the symbolism of
the birds themselves. For thousands of years the bird has been a symbol of the
human soul which, like a bird, can either be caged or fly free. The Persian title
– *Mantiq al-tair* – translates literally as *The Language* (or *Speech*) *of the Birds*,
and so it seems reasonable to conclude that Attar's birds give voice to the all-
too-human anxieties that arise when we embark on the inner journey. Such
anxieties are understandable, not least because they emanate from our ego-
centred self, which surely knows that the journey will culminate in its own
annihilation. Like the birds in Attar's poem we may be keen to embark on the
spiritual quest, but at a subconscious level we begin to have second thoughts
once we realize what it entails.

Attar understands our concerns. The individual birds not only represent
different personality types but they also embody the complex characteristics
which combine to make up the human individual. He chides the cowardly and
weak-willed, cajoles the indolent, deflates the arrogant and emboldens the
timid. He also provides a detailed map of the journey, in that the seven valleys
correspond to the seven stages of the Sufi Path, or the successive stages of the
human soul (the *nafs*) as it travels along the river of life towards the boundless
ocean. Today we might say, somewhat more prosaically, that Attar provides a
model for the evolution of individual human consciousness.

Attar's presentation of the Sufi Path in this allegorical form might have been influenced by a poem from the *Divan* of the poet Sana'i, in which the different bird calls are interpreted as the birds' way of praising God. He might also have been influenced by the collection of tales known as the *Fables of Bidpai* or *Kalila and Dimna*, in which the behaviour of animals and birds mimics that of human beings, usually with a moral purpose. A third work that could have influenced him was *The Bird* by the philosopher/physician Husayn ibn Sana (980–1037), better known in the West as Avicenna. Avicenna's treatise is a similar allegorization of the journey of the soul and involves a flock of birds flying over eight mountains on their journey to the 'Great King'. (Fariduddin Attar, *The Conference of the Birds*, tr. Afkham Darbandi and Dick Davis, 16)

In turn, Attar's *Conference of the Birds* appears to bear a close resemblance to certain medieval European works that appeared some time after it: for example, Chaucer's two works, the *Parliament of the Fowls* and the *Canterbury Tales* (in the latter, a group of pilgrims regale each other with stories), and Dante's *Divine Comedy*, with its similarly multi-layered allegory as well as its movement from the earthly to the divine realm. As its name suggests, John Bunyan's *Pilgrim's Progress* follows a similar format, while Boccaccio's *Decameron* (c.1350) comprises one hundred stories told by a group of people escaping from plague-stricken Florence. One of Attar's allegorical stories reappeared in a fifteenth-century chronicle in the guise of the tale of the Swiss national hero, William Tell, who refused to pay homage to the Austrian governor and was ordered to shoot an apple from his son's head with a crossbow. Out of interest, the story has been included below under the heading *The king and the slave*, as part of the hoopoe's response to the hawk's excuse as to why he will not make the journey to the Simurgh.

English translations of the *Conference* include a partial translation in couplets by Edward Fitzgerald (1889); a prose translation by C. S. Nott (1954) from a French translation by Garcin de Tassy (1863); and a complete translation in couplets by Afkham Darbandi and Dick Davis (1984). The following much abridged outline of the story is derived from these sources, with some additional commentary.

The Conference Opens
The hoopoe is elected
When the birds decide to set out on the quest for their true king they elect the

hoopoe to be their guide (*pir* or *shaykh*), for in the past he had been entrusted by King Solomon to carry messages to his beloved, the Queen of Sheba. The crest of feathers on the hoopoe's head is a sign that he has attained spiritual wisdom and on his beak he carries the word *Bismillah*, the first word of the Qur'an (meaning 'In the Name of God'). The hoopoe warns the birds that the journey ahead of them will be long and hard. To enter the Path they will need to abandon their former lives, but if they renounce them in the name of love the king they seek will give his life for them.

The birds make their excuses
No sooner has the hoopoe finished speaking than the birds start to make their excuses as to why they will not make the journey: the nightingale, parrot, peacock, duck, partridge, humay (a mythical bird), hawk, heron, owl, and finch all speak, followed by a joint complaint from the rest of the birds. Some of the birds thus named, such as the nightingale and the hawk, were already well established in the symbolic imagery of the Sufis at the time of Attar. In the case of the nightingale and the rose (*see below*), itself an evocative image, it is as though Attar is urging his audience to go beyond such imagery: to go in search of Real Love, not the emotional high. Other birds such as the duck and the parrot are linked with traditional Islamic themes appropriate to the characteristics of the individual birds. The duck's watery home is associated with the obligatory ablutions. The green of the parrot is associated with Khidr, a mysterious figure who is mentioned in the Qur'an and who appears in different guises and at different times to guide those in need. He is immortal, and has been likened to the Green Man of Western tradition.

The nightingale
As the hoopoe has just spoken to the birds about love, it seems appropriate that love should be the subject chosen by the nightingale: the first bird to make an excuse not to set out on the quest. He sings passionately of his knowledge of love's secrets, of how his song of love echoes through the dark night and is taken up in the lament of the lute and the haunting sound of the reed-flute. His love of the rose is such that he cannot bear to be parted from her, nor she from him. Only the rose understands the secret of his love, and his love for her is such that he gives no thought to his own existence. The

journey to the Simurgh is beyond him – the love of the rose is enough, because it is for the nightingale that the rose comes joyfully into bloom each year. How could he spend even a single night away from his beloved?

The nightingale personifies emotional love: the lover who is in love with being in love. The hoopoe chides him, telling him he is in love with the external, transient beauty of things. It is not true love, but delusion that causes him to have sleepless nights. And while he may think the joy of the rose is because it blooms *for* him, in reality she is laughing *at* him. The hoopoe then tells an allegorical story about a princess and a dervish to illustrate the nightingale's predicament. He responds in a similar vein to each bird as it presents its excuses: an admonishment followed by an allegorical story.

The parrot

Clothed in green, and with sugar in her beak, the parrot tells how men have shut her up in a cage. If she were free again, she would search out the spring guarded by Khidr, from which flow the waters of immortality. Like him she wears the colour green, for she is a Khidr among birds. She would be quite content to drink from his stream of ever-living water and has no desire to seek the Simurgh. The hoopoe tells her a story about Khidr, who wished to be friends with a fool in love with God. The fool of God – that is to say, a dervish – said that it would be an impossible friendship because Khidr was destined to live for ever, whereas he was mortal and born to die.

The peacock

Next comes the proud peacock who listened to the serpent and was expelled from Paradise, and to Paradise he wishes to return. He wishes for nothing more. The hoopoe tells him that the earthly paradise sought by the peacock is just a drop, whereas the whole ocean could be his. He should seek wholeness in the Whole.

The duck

The duck claims self-righteously that since she performs the obligatory ablutions day and night she is the purest and most devout bird that ever lived in either of the two worlds. Water is everything to her, so why should she care about the Simurgh?

The partridge

The self-satisfied partridge says that he spends his life searching for jewels on the mountainside – for him nothing else has the permanence of a precious stone, and he has become a slave to his search for them.

The humay

The mythical humay boasts that his shadow is a maker of kings and thrones, so why would he need to seek the Simurgh?

The hawk

The hawk sits on the wrists of kings and knows exactly how to behave in their company, even though he can see nothing because of the hood he wears over his eyes. He is content with life at court, and so even to dream of travelling in search of another king would be the height of folly. Life is so much better on a royal wrist than struggling through a dried up *wadi* (a watercourse that is dry in the summer).

In his reply, the hoopoe tells the hawk that he sets great store on superficial appearances. The Simurgh is unlike any worldly king for he rules alone and has no rivals for his throne. The rule of a true king is constant. A worldly king may often be just, but he can also be guilty of wrongdoing. The closer one is to a king, the more precarious one's position, and the more one is at risk from the king's displeasure. People say kings are like fire, and so it is best to keep one's distance from them. The hoopoe then tells the hawk a cautionary but familiar tale.

The king and the slave

There was once a certain king who had a favourite slave, a handsome young man, from whom he could not bear to be parted. The king showered him with gifts and was clearly devoted to him, but he was also in the habit of placing an apple on the young man's head and using it for target practice. One day a foolish courtier asked the slave why, when he was the king's favourite, did he quake and blanch with fear whenever the king loosed an arrow at the apple. The slave replied: 'If the king were to hit me instead of the apple, I would be blamed and dismissed as being worse than useless. It wouldn't matter whether I were dead or alive. But when the arrow splits the apple, people praise the king's skill. In my situation either the king is skilled, or the slave is killed!'

The heron
The melancholy heron tells how he prefers to be on the sea-shore where he can stand and contemplate the water. Although he haunts the water's edge, the ocean is not for him. He has not even drunk a single drop of it. The focus of his love is the ocean, against which he would find the glory of the Simurgh little comfort.

The owl
Wearing a bewildered expression on his face, the owl says he has chosen to frequent abandoned ruins to get away from the strife that accompanies human habitation. He hopes that in this way he will one day stumble across a forgotten treasure. His love is for the glory of buried gold, whereas the love for the Simurgh is but a fable.

The finch
The finch claims to be too weak and insignificant to undertake the journey to the Simurgh. Moreover she is afraid that she will die of exhaustion along the way, or end up turning to ashes under his all-consuming gaze. Instead she will remain behind and seek her beloved in a well, for that is where Joseph was found.

The rest of the birds now make their excuses, too. Attar, the narrator, asks us to excuse him for not repeating them all. There are so many, and they are all lame or inappropriate. The birds conclude by telling the hoopoe that it would be easier for them to make the journey if they knew there were some kind of connection between themselves and the Simurgh. The hoopoe explains that they are all shadows of the Simurgh. Heaven forbid them from taking this to mean that they are God; rather, that they are immersed in God. Although no one can see Him face to face, He has given them a mirror in which they can see His reflection. That mirror is their heart. If they seek Him there, they will see His image.

The hoopoe tells them another story to encourage them to continue with their journey. The story tells of the struggle between the heart and the lower self, a struggle that the heart wins. Inspired by the story, and the desire to be rid of the lower self, the birds decide to set off once more. They only travel a short way before they stop again, this time to elect a leader. They draw lots and, as chance would have it, the hoopoe wins. After hailing the hoopoe as their leader, thousands of birds fill the sky as they prepare to leave, but there are many more false starts. A change has come over the birds, however. They are no longer making excuses. Instead they ask questions about the Way that lies ahead of them, and each time the hoopoe responds with an appropriate story.

A bird complains about the self

One of the birds complains that he has a robber inside him, his lower self. He asks the hoopoe how he can continue the journey when he is dogged by the 'dog of desire' – a dog that will not obey him and is turning into a wolf. The hoopoe replies that the lower self grows as we grow, and as it grows it saps our spiritual strength. Unless we subdue our lower self we will get to the end of our lives with nothing except a desire for external things. We will have become a slave to our 'dog of desire'. The hoopoe then tells the story of a king and a dervish. The story was told in a slightly different form in the Introduction to this book but is repeated here because it may by now have taken on a different meaning for the reader.

The king and the Sufi

A king once encountered an old man dressed in rags. Not knowing him to be a follower of the Way of the Sufis, the king questioned him, saying: 'Who is the better of us, me or you?'

The old man replied, 'O ignorant one! Your words are as empty as your head. A Sufi does not normally sing his own praises but, since you oblige me to do so, let me tell you that one Sufi is worth a thousand men like you. Your ignorance of the Way has made you the slave of your conceited ego. You have been harnessed by it and it has made an ass of you, because you do whatever it tells you to do. Whoever follows the Way of Truth learns how to master his ego, and rides it like an ass. Now, since I have mastered what has mastered you, it should be obvious which one is the better of us. You are in love with your lower self. It has lit the fires of desire in you, and you are being burned alive in the flames.'

A *bird asks about a gift for the Simurgh*
When a bird asks what would be an appropriate gift to take the Simurgh, the hoopoe advises the bird to take something that would not be found at the court of the king. The things to be found at the court include knowledge, secrets, and an obedient soul. So the hoopoe suggests taking a heart filled with longing, and a soul in torment because these things are unknown there. If one sigh reaches the court from the innermost depths of the soul, that person will attain their goal. The hoopoe continues with the following story.

A *man asks for a prayer mat*
A man once asked the Prophet for a prayer mat. The Prophet replied: 'The sands of the desert are burning. Pray there, and press your forehead against the hot sand until you feel it sear your flesh. The mark left on your face will be a token of the wound within, since the hearts of all who have been wounded by love bear its scars. A scarred heart shows that one has pressed forward on the Way of Love.'

The First Valley, or the Valley of the Quest
The birds ask the hoopoe about the path that lies ahead of them, and he describes the Seven Valleys and what the traversing of each entails. The first valley, the Valley of the Quest, takes many years to pass through. There all sorts of difficulties and hardship will assail the birds until such time as they renounce the world and everything they possess. Freed from worldly desires, they will be able to devote themselves to the quest. When love begins to open their hearts they will ask the cup-bearer for some wine – just to taste what awaits them – and once they have drunk it nothing will matter except the quest. In the final state, they are prepared to wait for the door to be opened before they proceed. Their passage through the door brings to an end the existence of dogma, belief and unbelief.

Anecdotes of Majnun and Rabi'ah
To illustrate this stage of the journey the hoopoe tells the birds some more

stories, two of which were told earlier in this book: Majnun sifting the dust by the roadside in his search for Layla (page 84), and the anecdote behind Rabi'ah's comment: 'The door has never been shut' (page 94).

The Second Valley, or the Valley of Love
Here the seeker will be consumed by the flames of love in his/her desire to reach the Beloved. Whereas some might be deterred by Love's fire and turn back, nothing holds back true lovers. Duality has no hold over them: they have no time for doubt or certainty, good and evil are the same to them. True lovers do not hesitate. They will give up everything they own to spend just one moment in the Divine Presence. They are like a fish cast up on dry land by a wave: it will struggle with its whole being to return to the ocean. When love enters the heart, reason leaves the head. The eye of reason will never reveal the innermost secrets of life in the way that love can. Love leads seekers to the Path, and makes lovers impatient to be on their way.

The nobleman who loved a beer-seller
A nobleman left his family and sold everything he possessed – his house, belongings, and slaves – just so that he could buy beer from the young beer-seller with whom he had fallen in love. The poorer he became, the stronger his love grew for the young beer-seller. When he was destitute people gave him food, but as he had nothing left to sell he exchanged the food for beer. When someone asked him about the love that had reduced him to this pitiable state, he replied: 'Love is such that you will sell the world and everything in it a hundred times over, just to buy a drop of beer.' The hoopoe concludes the story by telling the birds that the nobleman's actions were a demonstration of the power of love. Unless they could match his ardour, they would never experience the depth of feeling love provokes. The hoopoe also tells them the story about Majnun and the sheepskin (see page 83).

The Third Valley, or the Valley of Understanding
Also described as the Valley of Mystic Apprehension or Gnosis, the Valley of Understanding has no beginning or end. Here every traveller takes a different route, gaining an understanding that is appropriate to their qualities and state. After all, could an ant or spider tread a path identical to that of the elephant,

or could a gnat outfly the wind? No one can ever know the inner path of another, for we each gain our insight and understanding in different ways: some find it in the prayer niche of a mosque, others at pagan shrines. But when the light of Truth illuminates his understanding, each seeker finds the particular path he is to follow. As his essence shines forth, the world that seemed before to be like a fiery furnace will become as sweet as paradise. One sees through the outer skin to the essence of things, and the sense of separation – of existing as a separate 'self' – will disappear, revealing the Divine Unity within every thing. Yet many have lost their way here. Seduced by their state, they thought they had arrived at their journey's end and so lost the zeal to continue. Even though you find yourself bathed in bliss, or even though you reach the throne of God, never forget to ask: 'Is there yet more?' Let your mind be drowned in the sea of knowledge. If you prefer to sleep, you will never see the Friend. Come! Persevere in the Path of Truth!

The lover who slept
Exhausted by love's tears and sighs, a troubled lover lay down on the ground and went to sleep. His beloved happened to pass by, and finding him fast asleep wrote a note which she pinned to his cloak. When he awoke and read the note his trouble returned, a thousand times worse than before. His beloved had written: 'If you are a merchant, stir yourself, for the market is open. If you are an ascetic, spend your nights in prayer. But if you are a lover, you should blush with shame. Sleep is not for lovers. By day they watch the wind blow; by night they observe the waxing and waning of the moon. But you do neither of these and so your love for me is untrue. A man who falls asleep before he is overtaken by death's slumber is a man in love with himself! You have no understanding of love, so may your sleep be like your ignorance – prolonged and deep!'

The Fourth Valley, or the Valley of Detachment
Understanding leads to the Valley of Detachment, where all desire and striving for meaning disappear. An icy wind blows through the soul, laying everything to waste – the seven oceans, the seven planets, and the arc of the heavens become a mere speck of dust. Even the fires of hell freeze over. More miraculous than this, a tiny ant is stronger than an elephant here; and while a

raven fills its crop, countless caravans of souls will perish. A hundred thousand angels wept when the light that dispels all darkness shone forth from Adam; a hundred thousand creatures drowned in the waters when Noah built the ark; as many gnats were sent to quell an army so that Abraham could defeat Nimrod; a similar number of first-born children were slain before Moses was able to see God; as many took to Christianity when Jesus saw the hidden mystery of God; as many met their fate before Muhammad's night journey took him up to heaven's gate. If you were to see the whole world go up in flames, it would be but a dream compared to Reality. If thousands of souls were to die, they would be like a drop of dew absorbed into the ocean. If heaven and earth were to come to an end, a grain of sand will have been lost.

The hoopoe intersperses his description of the valley with stories, each of which is told with a view to decreasing the birds' attachment to the phenomenal world. He tells them: 'You have to abandon your trivial pursuits and pursue what is essential in life. You will need to work at it, but not in the manner in which you are used to working. What you have done in the past needs to be forgotten. Instead you must learn how to tell what work needs to be done and what needs to be shunned. Act with detachment in everything. Detachment is like a firestorm, reducing a hundred worlds to ashes. The whole of creation disappears in the Valley of Detachment. What is there left to be afraid of if the world is no more?

The fly and the honey

A hungry fly saw a beehive in a garden. Carried away by thoughts of the delicious honey, he said: 'I will give a grain of barley to whoever helps me get into the hive.' A passer-by felt pity for the fly and placed him in the hive. But when he got to the honey he found that his wings and legs stuck to it. His struggle to free himself only made things worse. Exhausted, he cried out: 'This honey is poisonous. I didn't know how lucky I was when I was free. Now I'm well and truly snared. I gave a barley grain to get in here, but I would gladly give two to get out.'

The hoopoe adds that no one can be free in this valley. Yet only those who have reached the necessary degree of spiritual maturity are able to pass through it into a new life. The valley awaits. So give up the selfish ego and all its attachments. It is a pagan idol, a deceptive guide.

The Fifth Valley, or the Valley of Unity

The hoopoe says of this valley that however things may appear, whether many or few, they are all one. Unit and number are no more. Forget 'forever' and the day the world began. Those days are gone. So is eternity.

The dervish and the world of wax

A dervish was asked about the nature of the world. He replied: 'The phenomenal world is like a child's multicoloured toy – say, a palm-tree – which is made of wax. If you knead the tree in your hand, the many forms and colours become a lump of wax again. What appeared to be many is only one, not two. If there is nonduality, there cannot be duality. There is no "I" and "thou".'

A lover rescues his beloved

A young woman fell into a river. As quick as a flash her lover dived in to save her, swimming against the current until he reached her side. When they were safely on the bank again, she said: 'I fell in by accident, but why did you come in after me and risk your life too?'

Her lover replied: 'I dived in after you because in lovers' eyes there is no "I" and "you". For a long time we were separate, but now when we are together I am you and you are me. So why talk of us as "two"?'

To talk of two creates duality. When the two disappear there is Unity.

The Sixth Valley, or the Valley of Astonishment

This valley is a place of pain and sadness, where each breath is a sigh, and each sigh is so like a thrusting sword that you wish death would hasten. In your bewilderment the Unity you knew is gone. If someone asks how you are, you reply: 'Who am I to say? I know nothing with certainty any more. I even doubt my own doubt. I am in love, but with whom? My heart is empty, yet at the same time it is filled with love.'

The lost key

A dervish heard a voice cry out: 'I've lost my key. If anybody finds it, please give it back to me. My door is locked, and I'm outside in the road. If my door remains locked, how will I get back in?'

The dervish said to him: 'What do you have to complain about? You know where your door is. Even though it is locked, if you remain outside it long enough someone will eventually open it for you. You may think you have problems, but I've lost both the key and the door!'

The hoopoe comments that people cannot understand the plight of the dervish and the profound state of bewilderment in which he finds himself. When people ask you 'What can I do?' then say to them 'Change your ways. Bid farewell to your actions and reactions of the past.' Whoever enters the Valley of Astonishment will be bewildered with sorrow. He will think he has lost the Way. The sure knowledge he had will turn to indecision and fear.

The Seventh Valley, or the Valley of Poverty and Annihilation

Words cannot describe the next and last valley, for here the mind has gone. All is forgotten. When a ray of celestial sunlight penetrates its atmosphere, the myriad shadows that surround you disappear. When the ocean heaves, nothing can save the patterns playing on the surface of each wave. This disintegrating pattern symbolizes the impermanence of the two worlds, and yet people want it to endure. Whoever merges with the ocean and sinks into its depths will be blessed with eternal peace and tranquillity. And if he should emerge from this state he will know the secrets of creation.

Because everyone disappears in the end, it may be thought that they are all alike – just as twigs and incense are reduced to identical-looking ash when burnt. Yet although outwardly they seem to be the same, inwardly they are different. When an impure soul sinks into the ocean it retains its impure state. But when a purified soul sinks into the ocean it will lose its separate identity and become one with the ocean and its movement. It is non-existent, yet it exists. How can this be? It is a state the mind cannot conceive.

The moths and the flame

One night some moths were brought together by a desire to learn the truth about the candle's light. They decided that one of them should go and explore the candle's elusive flame. So a moth flew off and eventually came to a palace where he saw a light burning in a window. He flew back to tell the others, according to his understanding, what he had discovered. A wise moth who was presiding over the gathering dismissed his findings, saying: 'He knows nothing of the flame.' A second moth flew off and fluttered ever closer to the fire, touching it with the tip of his wing, but the heat was too much for him. When he reported back to the other moths what he had discovered about the flame, the wise moth remarked: 'You do not bear the marks of one who has fathomed the secret of the candle's flame.' A third moth set off. Intoxicated with love, he wooed the flame before throwing himself into its fire. He embraced the flame and then was engulfed by her so that flame and moth were united. Watching from afar, the wise moth saw the sudden blaze, and said: 'He has learnt the truth about the flame. But only he knows that of which we cannot speak.'

The Journey

When he had finished describing the seven valleys, the hoopoe paused. His audience was filled with fear, for they realized what a daunting undertaking the path would be. Some of them died of despair there and then. The remainder set off on their journey. The greater part of their lives passed them by in the years they spent flying over mountains and valleys until, at last, they reached their journey's end. Attar says that he cannot tell us what happened to them along the way, but that if we ever travel the same Path we will experience for ourselves what they went through.

The birds arrive and are greeted by a herald

Of the many hundreds of thousands of birds that had set out, only thirty remained when they arrived at the promised goal. Thirty exhausted, bedraggled birds. They are greeted by a herald who launches a barrage of questions at them and then tells them that they are not worthy of entering into the presence of the king. His advice to them is to retrace their path. But the birds will not be put off by the herald. They persist, citing as evidence of their state some of the stories they heard along the way about love, lover and the Beloved. When the herald warns them that the glory of the king's majesty reduces souls to nought, they ask him how a moth can turn back from the flame when its desire is to be united with the fire. Having tested the birds, the herald eventually opens the door for them. What happened next is told in Edward Fitzgerald's nineteenth-century rendering of the story.

Then cried the Spokesman, 'Be it even so:
Let us but see the Fount from which we flow,
And, seeing, lose Ourselves therein!' And, Lo!
Before the Word was utter'd, or the Tongue
Of Fire replied, or Portal open flung,
They were *within* – they were before the *Throne*,
Before the Majesty that sat thereon,
But wrapt in so insufferable a Blaze
Of Glory as beat down their baffled Gaze,
Which, downward drooping, fell upon a Scroll
That, Lightning-like, flash'd back on each the whole
Past half-forgotten Story of his Soul:
Like that which Yusuf (Joseph) in his Glory gave
His brethren as some Writing he would have
Interpreted; and at a Glance, behold
Their own Indenture for their Brother sold!
And so with these poor Thirty: who abasht
In Memory all laid bare and Conscience lasht,
By full Confession and Self-loathing flung
The Rags of carnal Self that round them clung;
And, their old selves self-knowledged and self-loathed,
And in the Soul's Integrity re-clothed,
Once more they ventured from the Dust to raise
Their Eyes – up to the Throne – into the Blaze,
And in the Centre of the Glory there
Beheld the Figure of – *Themselves* as 't were
Transfigured – looking to Themselves, beheld
The Figure on the Throne en-miracled,
Until their Eyes themselves and *That* between
Did hesitate which *Seer* was, which *Seen*;
They That, That They: Another, yet the Same;
Dividual, yet One: from where there came
A Voice of awful Answer, scarce discern'd
From *which* to Aspiration *whose* return'd
They scarcely knew; as when some Man apart

Answers aloud the Question in his Heart –
The Sun of my Perfection is a Glass
Wherein from *Seeing* into *Being* pass
All who, reflecting as reflected see
Themselves in Me, and Me in Them; not Me,
But all of Me that a contracted Eye
Is comprehensive of Infinity:
Nor yet *Themselves*; no Selves, but of The All
Fractions, from which they split and whither fall.
As Water lifted from the Deep, again
Falls back in individual Drops of Rain
Then melts into the Universal Main.
All you have been, and seen, and done, and thought
Not *You* but *I*, have seen and been and wrought:
I was the Sin that from Myself rebell'd:
I was the Remorse that tow'rd Myself compelled:
I was the Tajidar who led the Track:
I was the little Briar that pull'd you back:
Sin and Contrition – Retribution owed,
And cancell'd – Pilgrim, Pilgrimage, and Road,
Was but Myself toward Myself: and Your
Arrival but *Myself* at my own Door:
Who in your Fraction of Myself behold
Myself within the Mirror Myself hold
To see Myself in, and each part of Me
That sees himself, though drown'd, shall ever see.
Come you lost Atoms to your Centre draw,
And be the Eternal Mirror that you saw:
Rays that have wander'd into Darkness wide
Return, and back into your Sun subside.

Ibn 'Arabi and *The Treatise on Being*

> When the mystery of the oneness of the soul and the Divine is revealed
> to you, you will understand that you are no other than God. . . . Then
> you will see all your actions to be His actions and all your attributes to
> be His attributes and your essence to be His essence.

Ibn 'Arabi's influence on his own and subsequent generations of Sufis is such that he is known as the *Shaykh al-Akbar* – the Greatest Shaykh, or Teacher. His influence was not confined to Islam, however, for he was known to the Christian West as 'Doctor Maximus', a literal translation of his Arabic title. In contrast to Fariduddin Attar, whose teaching and expression of Sufi principles were accomplished largely through anecdotal stories, the majority of Ibn 'Arabi's prolific writings are more mystical or philosophical in tone. An intellectual giant, the universality of his writings and teachings is captured in one of his poems.

> My heart has become capable of every form:
> It is a pasture for gazelles,
> A monastery for Christian monks,
> A temple for idols,
> The pilgrim's Ka'ba
> The tablets of the Torah,
> And the Book of the Qur'an.
> I follow the religion of Love:
> Whatever way Love's camel takes,
> That is my religion and my faith.

The Early Years

When Ibn 'Arabi was born in Murcia in 1165, southern Spain had been an Arab country for over 400 years. He is said to have come into the world on the twenty-seventh day of the month of Ramadan, traditionally regarded as the Night of Power, of which the Qur'an says: '. . . the Night of Power is better than a thousand months. On that night the angels and the Spirit descend . . . ' (97:3–4) His father was a follower of 'Abdul-Qadir Gilani and the young Ibn 'Arabi was brought up in an environment frequented by the Sufi friends of his parents. In 1173, when he was eight years old, his family moved to Seville where he studied the Qur'an, the Sunnah of the Prophet Muhammad and the *shari'ah*. While he was still young he was instructed in the religious sciences by two elderly women mystics: Shams of Marchena and Fatima of Cordova. He wrote about the latter in *Sufis of Andalusia*.

> I served as a disciple one of the lovers of God, a gnostic, a lady of Seville called Fatimah bint Ibn al-Muthanna of Cordova. I served her for several years, she being over ninety-five years of age . . . She used to play on the tambourine and show great pleasure in it. When I spoke to her about it she answered, 'I take joy in Him Who has turned to me and made me one of His Friends (Saints), using me for His own purposes. Who am I that He should choose me among mankind? He is jealous of me for, whenever I turn to something other than He in heedlessness, He sends me some affliction concerning that thing.' . . .With my own hands I built for her a hut of reeds as high as she, in which she lived until she died.
> (Ibn 'Arabi, *Sufis of Andalusia*, 25–26)

From an early age, Ibn 'Arabi practised meditation, prayer and fasting. He also studied alchemy, astrology, the Hermetic tradition and Neo-Platonic philosophy. When he was nineteen, he met the philosopher Ibn Rushd (d.1198) – known to the West as Averroes – who asked him a searching question: 'Do the fruits of mystic illumination agree with philosophical speculation?' 'Yes and no', replied Ibn 'Arabi. 'Between the Yea and the Nay the spirits take their flight beyond matter.' Ibn Rushd was so impressed by this response that he later confided to friends: 'Glory to Allah that I have lived at a time when there exists a master of this experience, one of those who opens the locks of His doors. Glory to Allah that I was granted the gift of seeing one of them myself.' When Ibn Rushd died fourteen years later, Ibn 'Arabi attended his funeral and wrote: 'This is the *iman* (leader) and these his works; would that I knew whether his hopes were realized.' (Ibn 'Arabi, *The Seals of Wisdom*, 19, 20)

Meetings with Khidr

We are told that Ibn 'Arabi met Khidr, the immortal guide, three times. On the first occasion Ibn 'Arabi had disagreed over some points of doctrine with his teacher, Shaykh 'Abdul Hassan. That night, while he was asleep, Khidr appeared to him in a dream and said: 'The things that your teacher told you were right – accept them.' Ibn 'Arabi awoke from the dream and immediately rushed off to tell 'Abdul Hassan. His teacher, who showed no surprise at being disturbed by his pupil in the middle of the night, explained that he had appealed to Khidr to correct his brilliant but obstinate pupil. On hearing this, Ibn 'Arabi vowed never to disagree with him again.

The second meeting occurred one night while Ibn 'Arabi was on board a ship, during a visit to Tunisia. Unable to sleep, he was walking about on the deck when he espied a figure striding across the water towards him. Khidr strode up to the side of the boat, conversed briefly with Ibn 'Arabi, then turned around, and in three giant strides he disappeared over the horizon. Although he never revealed the subject of their conversation, Ibn 'Arabi reported that the next morning he was walking through the streets of Tunis when an elderly shaykh approached him and enquired about his meeting of the night before with Khidr.

The third encounter took place in a mosque in Andalusia. Ibn 'Arabi was addressing an audience on the role of creative imagination in the manifestation of so-called miracles. Some of those present rejected his proposition that the purified mind could produce such phenomena. While they were objecting, Khidr entered the mosque. Unrecognized by all but Ibn 'Arabi, he unrolled his prayer mat and suddenly ascended five metres into the air. Having said his prayers, he descended gently to the ground and left. The objections had been overruled. (Ibn 'Arabi, *The Seals of Wisdom*, 19–20)

Mecca and Damascus

The early years of Ibn 'Arabi's life were mainly spent in Andalusia and North Africa. It was while he was in Morocco in 1200 that he had a vision in which he was told to go to Fez, where he would meet a certain Muhammad al-Hasar with whom he would travel east. The two men duly met and journeyed together to Tunis, Alexandria and Cairo, where Ibn 'Arabi's travelling companion died. From Cairo Ibn 'Arabi travelled on alone to Mecca, where he was welcomed into a small group of mystics. In the group was a young woman who was to make a profound and enduring impression upon him. Ibn 'Arabi wrote:

> This shaykh had a daughter, a slender child who captivated all who saw her, whose mere presence embellished any gathering, and who filled with wonder anyone who beheld her. Her name was Nizam (Harmony) and her surname 'Eye of the Sun and Beauty' (*'ayn al-Shams wa'l-Baha'*). She was wise and pious, having had experience of the spiritual and mystical life; she personified the august seniority of the entire Holy Land and the artless youth of the great city of the Prophet . . . If it were not for small-minded souls, quick to make accusations of scandal and with a predisposition for malicious gossip, I would comment here upon the beauty with which God endowed her body as well as her soul, the latter being a garden of plenitude . . .
>
> (Quoted in Henry Corbin, *L'Imagination Créatrice dans le Soufisme d'Ibn 'Arabi*, 110–111, tr. John Baldock)

Nizam was the inspiration behind a volume of love poetry – *Tarjuman al-Ashwaq* (*The Interpreter of Desires*) – completed by Ibn 'Arabi in about 1215, which was to cause problems for him with the religious orthodoxy. As he explained in his major work *The Meccan Revelations*, which he began to write while in Mecca, if you love another being for their beauty 'you love none other than God, for He is *the* Beautiful Being. Thus in all its aspects, the object of love is God alone.' In the preface to his collection of love poems, he wrote:

> Whatever name I mention in this work, it is to her I am alluding. Whichever dwelling I eulogise, it is her dwelling that is in my mind. But there is more. In the verses I composed for the present volume, I never cease to allude to the divine inspirations, the

spiritual visitations, the correspondences (in our world) with the world of Angelic Intelligences. This was to conform to my customary manner of thinking in symbols, which is because the things of the invisible world hold a greater attraction for me than the things of this present life, and because this young girl knew perfectly well to what I was alluding (that is, the esoteric meaning of my verses).

(Quoted in Henri Corbin, *L'Imagination Créatrice dans le Soufisme d'Ibn 'Arabi*, 111, tr. John Baldock)

In spite of this, and the warning to his readers not to be tempted into thinking that his poems were about base things, he was accused of writing erotic poetry. In his own defence, he later wrote a commentary on the poems to show that the imagery was compatible with orthodox Islam. (The inspiration Ibn 'Arabi found in Nizam is often compared to that which Dante found in his beloved Beatrice.)

Ibn 'Arabi travelled to Baghdad in 1204 and Cairo in 1206, where he was greeted with open hostility by the orthodox religionists. After a friend had saved him from arrest and possible execution, he travelled north to Aleppo and Konya in Anatolia. There he married the mother of Sadr al-Din al-Qunawi, one of his closest followers – who later sat at the feet of Jalaluddin Rumi. After making further journeys, he received an invitation to move to Damascus, where he settled in 1223, teaching and writing until his death in 1240.

Shortly before he died, Ibn 'Arabi enraged some theologians when he confronted them, saying: 'What you worship is under my feet.' His tomb was destroyed after his death and the spot where the confrontation had taken place was dug up to reveal a cache of gold coins.

The Writings of Ibn 'Arabi

Ibn 'Arabi is said to have written between 250 and 300 books: the breadth of his intellect and vision is so vast that we can only touch on the surface of it here. A number of themes run through his writings, the most significant of which is 'the Oneness of Being' (*wahdat al-wujud*), also referred to as the 'Unity of Being'. While we might be able to grasp this as a spiritual concept, in his *Meccan Revelations* Ibn 'Arabi stresses that this state of unity, like other mystical states, has to be experienced to be understood:

> Knowledge of mystical states can only be had by actual experience, nor can the reason of man define it, nor arrive at any cognizance of it by deduction, as is also the case with knowledge of the taste of honey, the bitterness of patience, the bliss of sexual union, love, passion or desire, all of which cannot possibly be known unless one is properly qualified or experiences them directly.
>
> (*The Seals of Wisdom*, 21)

A further theme in Ibn 'Arabi's work is the 'Perfect Man' (*al-Insan al-kamil*) – the word 'Man' here includes both women and men. Having realized his/her full potential as a human being, Perfect Man embodies the Real and thus serves as a bridge or isthmus (*barzakh*) between the two worlds: heaven and earth, or Divine and human. In fact it is the 'heart' of Perfect Man which is the isthmus, for it has been polished to such a degree that it conforms to the *hadith qudsi*: 'My Earth and My Heaven containeth me not, but the heart of My faithful servant containeth me.'

The following extracts from Ibn 'Arabi's writings are confined to three of his works: *The Bezels of Wisdom*, *The Kernel of the Kernel*, and the *Treatise on Being*.

The Bezels of Wisdom (Fusus al-Hikam)

The *Fusus al-Hikam*, written in about 1230, is often regarded as Ibn 'Arabi's spiritual testament and a crystallization of his teaching. The symbolic significance of the title, which translates literally as 'the settings of the Wisdom', is explained by Titus Burckhardt: *fusus* derives from the setting which holds a precious stone or seal in place in a ring; *al-hikam* refers to aspects of the Divine Wisdom. Thus 'the "settings" which hold the precious stones of the eternal Wisdom (*al-hikmah*) are the spiritual "forms" of different Prophets, their respective natures, both human and spiritual, which transport such or such an aspect of the Divine Knowledge. The incorruptible character of the precious stone corresponds to the unchanging nature of Wisdom.' (Ibn 'Arabi, *The Wisdom of the Prophets*, 1–2)

The *Fusus al-Hikam* comprises twenty-seven chapters, each of which bears the name of one of the Prophets, culminating with the Prophet Muhammad, the Seal of the Prophets. The titles of some of the chapters are:

> The Divine Wisdom in the Word of Adam
> The Wisdom of the Divine Inspiration in the Word of Seth
> The Wisdom of the Transcendence in the Word of Noah
> The Wisdom of Holiness in the Word of Enoch
> The Wisdom of Rapturous Love in the Word of Abraham
> The Wisdom of the Truth in the Word of Isaac
> The Sublime Wisdom in the Word of Ismaël
> The Illuminated Wisdom in the Word of Joseph
> The Wisdom of the Heart in the Word of Shu'aib
> The Wisdom of the Destiny in the Word of Ezra
> The Wisdom of the Prophecy in the Word of Jesus
> The Wisdom of the Merciful Beatitude in the Word of Solomon
> The Sublime Wisdom in the Word of Moses
> The Wisdom of the Singularity in the Word of Muhammad

From The Wisdom of the Transcendence in the Word of Noah

> For those who truly know *ahl al-haqaiq*, the Divine Realities, affirmation of transcendence imposes conditionality and limitation on the Real, for he who asserts that Deity is purely transcendent is either ignorant or tactless. The exotericist who stresses only Divine Transcendence (*at-tanzih*) slanders and misrepresents the Real and all the messengers, albeit unwittingly. He imagines that he has hit on the truth, whilst he has missed the mark, being like those who believe in part and deny in part.
>
> . . . one who draws comparisons with Deity without taking into consideration His incomparability restricts and limits Him and therefore does not know Him. He, however, who unites in his knowledge of Deity both transcendence and immanence in a universal way, even though it is not possible to know such a thing in detail because of the infinitude of cosmic forms, nevertheless

knows Him in a general way, just as he may know himself generally but not in detail. Thus the Prophet said, 'Who knows himself knows his Lord', linking together knowledge of God and knowledge of the self. In the Qur'an God says, *We will show them our signs on the horizons, meaning the world outside you, and in yourselves,* 'self' here meaning your inner essence, *until it becomes clear to them that All is the Real*, in that you are His form and He is your Spirit. You are in relation to Him as your physical form is to you. He is in relation to you as the governing spirit is to your physical form. This definition takes account of your outer and inner aspects, for the form that remains when the governing spirit is no longer present may no longer be called a man, but only a form having human appearance, there being no real distinction between it and the form of wood or stone. The name 'man' may be given to such a form only figuratively by extension, but not properly.

. . . Just as the outer form of Man gives praise with its tongue to its spirit and the soul that rules it, so also the cosmic forms glorify Him, although we cannot understand their praise because of our inability to comprehend all the forms of the Cosmos. All things are 'tongues' of the Real, giving expression to the praise of the Real. (*The Seals of Wisdom*, 47–8)

From The Sublime Wisdom in the Word of Moses

The prophets use a concrete language because they address themselves to the collectivity and they trust in the comprehension of the wise one who will hear them. If they talk figuratively, it is because of the ordinary people and because they know the degree of intuition of those who really know. It is thus that the Prophet said, in speaking of generosity, that he gave nothing to certain people who were more dear to him than others, for fear that God would throw them into the eternal fire. He expressed himself thus for the feeble minded who is a slave to avidity and natural inclinations.

In the same way, all that the prophets brought of sciences is clothed in forms which are accessible to the most ordinary intellectual capacities, so that he who does not go to the heart of things stops at this clothing and takes it for that which is the most beautiful, whereas the man of subtle comprehension, the diver who fishes the pearls of Wisdom, knows how to indicate for what reason such or such a Divine Truth is clothed in terrestrial form; he evaluates the robe and the material of which it is made, and knows by that, all that it covers, attaining thus to a science which remains inaccessible to those who do not have knowledge of this order.

Since the prophets, their messengers and their heirs know that there are in the world and in their own communities men who possess this intuition, they rely in their demonstrations on a concrete language equally accessible to the élite as to the common man, so that the man of the élite can gain at the same time that which the ordinary man gains and more, according to the measure in which the term of 'chosen' (khass) is applied really to him and distinguishes him from the blind man; and it is by that (by his intuitive understanding) that the wise are distinguished . . .
(*The Wisdom of the Prophets*, 106)

The Kernel of the Kernel (Lubbu-l-Lubb)

The Kernel of the Kernel is described as 'an intimate exposition of practical development in the Sufi tradition for reaching the state of *arif billah* (gnostic in God)'. In it Ibn 'Arabi describes the various stations, presences, and journeys that a person will encounter along the way to becoming a Perfect or Universal Man (*al-insan al-kamil*).

In the text immediately preceding the first of the following extracts, Ibn 'Arabi has described a human being as a 'Divine workhouse', subject to constant revelation of the Divine. Like the Divine itself, the Divine descent is colourless and formless. Yet God creates the revelations in colour and kind according to the colour of man, his belief, his inner being and his way of thinking. In this way the immanent quality of Reality (*haqq*) becomes self-explanatory. The spiritually mature person endeavours to return the Divine revelation in the same state that it came to him/her – that is, without form or weight, and colourless. Yet whatever we do, think, believe, or imagine affects the revelation. Our task is to return it exactly as it came. He continues:

> Whether it be in the man or outside him, all affairs, thoughts, actions, beliefs, imaginings and even all the breaths taken, not one atom of these things goes to naught. Every action, be it good or bad, has an ability and an aptitude according to itself, and they each take a form according to their state. And in the other universe they appear in the images they received here. The owner of those affairs and those actions, when he reaches them, in accordance to the image he gave them, he either finds bounty and dives into pleasure, or he is hurt and suffers. That which is secret here become [sic] open there. The meaning of the Quranic verse explains this: 'If a person has done good the size of an atom, he will see that; if he has done ill the size of an atom he will see that.'
> (*The Kernel of the Kernel*, 44)

> *The Perfect Man is such a pure, clean, absolute mirror that God, who is Absolute Beauty, sees His Ipseity* [Selfhood] *unconditionally therein.*

> The mirror of the Perfect Man is according to the revelation of God. The revelation which happens in others is according to the servant's imagination, his capacity to receive and his aptitude. God speaks the truth and guides to the straight path.
> (*The Kernel of the Kernel*, 46)

> According to the gnostic, what is seen in the mirrors of the two universes is one face. Even though it is like this each gnostic has attained to one perfection.
>
> Some of them say: 'At the end of it all there is nothing in which I do not see the Ipseity of God.'
>
> Another group says: 'There is nothing within which I do not see the Ipseity of God.'
>
> Another group says: 'I see Him before anything else.'
>
> Yet another group says: 'Only God.'

A certain group of gnostics say: 'Only God sees God.'

In this matter of seeing, five forms have occurred. The gnostic, after having gathered all these five in himself, finds that five other things happen, the explanation of which is not suitable here, and to reveal this even is forbidden. Those who want to find out let them hang onto the hem of a Perfect person and ask of him, because: 'The one who has not tasted cannot know;' this is a necessary condition. The rest cannot be explained by writing.

(*The Kernel of the Kernel*, 48)

The Treatise on Being (Risale-t-ul-wujudiyyah)

The following extracts are taken from Ibn 'Arabi's commentary on the *hadith*: 'Whoso knoweth himself knoweth his Lord.' In the first of the five passages, Ibn 'Arabi emphasizes that there is nothing other than God, and so we have no existence apart from Him. To know this is to know ourselves, and also to know God. In the second passage he points out the error of those who think that we somehow have to cease to exist in order to know God, for this implies that things have an existence that is 'other' than God, which is polytheism. The third and fourth passages express the underlying Unity of Being. The fifth extract opens with two *ahadith* favoured by the Sufis. The first – 'Die before you die' – is the essence of *islam*. An alternative rendering of the second, which is a Divine Tradition (*hadith qudsi*), is: 'When I love my servant . . . I become the hearing with which he hears, the seeing with which he sees, the hand with which he grasps, the feet with which he walks, the tongue with which he speaks.' The concluding idea that knowing ourselves – what we would call 'self-knowledge' – occurs when the ego is no more, may be a difficult one to take on board in the current spiritual climate prevailing in the West. Much of today's popular self-development work tends to inflate the ego rather than diminish it, thereby inadvertently reinforcing our sense of separation from the Divine Unity. Ibn 'Arabi's commentary is a useful antidote to this.

> . . . The Prophet (upon whom be peace) said: 'Whoso knoweth himself knoweth his Lord.' And he said (upon him be peace): 'I

know my Lord by my Lord.' The Prophet (upon whom be peace) points out by that, that thou art not thou: thou art He, without thou; not He entering into thee, nor thou entering into Him. And it is not meant by that, that thou art aught that exists . . . but it is meant by it that thou never wast nor wilt be, whether by thyself or through Him or in Him or along with Him. Thou art neither ceasing to be nor still existing. *Thou art He*, without one of these limitations. Then if thou know thine existence thus, then thou knowest God; and if not, then not.

('*Whoso Knoweth Himself* . . .', 4–5)

And most of 'those who know God' (*al 'urraf*) make a ceasing of existence and the ceasing of that ceasing a condition of attaining the knowledge of God, and that is an error and a clear oversight. . . . For things have no existence, and what does not exist cannot cease to exist. For the ceasing to be implies the positing of existence, and that is polytheism. Then if thou know thyself without existence or ceasing to be, then thou knowest God; and if not then not.

('*Whoso Knoweth Himself* . . .', 5)

When the mystery of the oneness of the soul and the Divine is revealed to you, you will understand that you are no other than God. . . . Then you will see all your actions to be His actions and all your attributes to be His attributes and your essence to be His essence.

 . . . Thus, instead of [your own] essence, there is the essence of God and in place of [your own] attributes there are the attributes of God. He who knows himself sees his whole existence to be the Divine existence, but does not experience that any change has taken place in his own nature or qualities. For when you know yourself, your sense of a limited identity vanishes, and you know that you and God are one and the same.

(Rom Landau, *The Philosophy of Ibn 'Arabi*, 83–84)

. . . There is no existence save His existence. . . . This means that
the existence of the beggar is His existence and the existence of
the sick is His existence. Now, when this is admitted, it is
acknowledged that all existence is His existence; and that the
existence of all created things, both accidents and substances, is His
existence; and when the secret of one particle of the atoms is clear,
the secret of all created things, both outward and inward, is clear;
and you do not see in this world or the next, anything except God.
(Rom Landau, *The Philosophy of Ibn 'Arabi*, 83)

. . . And so the Prophet (may God bless him and give him peace)
said, 'Die before ye die,' that is, know yourselves before ye die.
And he (upon whom be peace) said: 'God (whose name be
exalted) has said: The worshipper does not cease to draw near to
Me with good works until I love him. Then, when I love him, I am
to him hearing and sight and tongue and hand unto the end,'
pointing to the fact that he who knows himself sees his whole
existence to be His existence, and does not see any change take
place in his own essence or attributes, seeing that he was not the
existence of his essence, but was merely ignorant of the knowledge
of himself. For when thou 'knowest thyself,' thine egoism is taken
away, and thou knowest that thou art not other than God. For, if
thou hadst had an independent existence, so that thou didst not
require to cease to be or to 'know thyself,' then thou wouldest be
a Lord beside Him; and God forbid that He should have created a
Lord beside Himself.

The profit of the knowledge of the soul is, that thou
understandest and art sure that thy existence is neither existent nor
non-existent, and that thou are not, wast not, and never wilt be.
(*'Whoso Knoweth Himself . . .'*, 12–13)

Rumi and the
Mathnawi

> I have put duality away. I have seen that the two worlds are one;
> One I seek. One I know. One I see. One I call.
> (Nicholson, *Selected Poems From the Divani Shamsi Tabriz,* XXXI)

Mevlana Jalaluddin Rumi is without doubt the Sufi who is best known in the West, largely through the popularity of his passionate poetry on the theme of love and his association with the Mevlevis – the so-called 'Whirling Dervishes' – the Sufi Order named after him. (The honorific title 'Mevlana' means 'Our Master'.) In view of the predominantly materialistic outlook of the West, the popularity of Rumi's poetry is in some ways surprising for it is essentially mystical poetry, an expression of our intimate relationship with a Reality of a spiritual rather than material nature. It would thus seem to resonate with a deep-seated need that remains unfulfilled by the external paraphernalia of our modern lifestyle.

From Balkh to Konya

Jalaluddin Rumi was born in 1207 in Balkh in the province of Khorasan in northern Persia, where his father Baha'uddin Walad was a respected scholar and mystic. In 1219, with the Mongol hordes scything their way towards Khorasan, Jalaluddin's family left Balkh and travelled westwards. Tradition relates that the travellers passed through Nishapur, where they visited Fariduddin Attar. Attar was deeply impressed by the young Jalaluddin and presented him with a copy of his *Asrar-nama* (Book of Secrets). As Baha'uddin set off again with Jalaluddin following behind, Attar is said to have remarked: 'There goes a river dragging a mighty ocean behind it.'

They journeyed on to Baghdad, Mecca, Jerusalem, Damascus and Aleppo before coming to Laranda (Karaman) in the central Anatolian province of Rum (that is, 'Roman' Anatolia, from which is derived the name 'Rumi') where Baha'uddin was invited to teach in the *madrasa* founded by the local governor. It was here that Jalaluddin, now aged 18, was married, and his first son – named Sultan Walad in honour of his grandfather – was born. Here, too, Jalaluddin's mother and his elder brother 'Ala'uddin both died.

While in Laranda, Baha'uddin received an invitation from the Seljuk ruler of Rum to teach in Konya (ancient Iconium in Galatia, which had been visited by St. Paul), the provincial capital of Rum. It was at about this time that Jalaluddin's second son was born, named 'Ala'uddin after his uncle, who had died in Laranda.

Baha'uddin Walad died in the January of 1231, leaving behind him the *Ma'arif*, a collection of writings in which, among other things, he described his spiritual experiences. According to Dr Annemarie Schimmel, the author of many books on Rumi and Sufism, Baha'uddin 'experienced the highest mystical states as utterly sensual, as a veritable consummation of love in God's embrace, and he recognized this loving activity of God, His "being with" everything (*mai'yyat*) in the life of everything created.' (Schimmel, *Rumi's World*, 14)

Burhanuddin Muhaqqiq

Shortly after Baha'uddin's death one of his former pupils from Khorasan, Burhanuddin Muhaqqiq, arrived in Konya. He met Jalaluddin and took charge of his spiritual development, instructing him in the spiritual practices of the Sufis and introducing him to the work of the Sufi poet Sana'i who had been the first to use the *mathnawi* (rhyming couplet) form as a vehicle for spiritual expression and instruction. Burhanuddin also sent Jalaluddin to Aleppo and Damascus, where it is possible that he met the great Andalusian Sufi, Ibn 'Arabi, who spent his last years in Damascus, dying there in 1240. It was around this same year that Burhanuddin left Konya for Kayseri (ancient Caesarea), where he spent the remainder of his life.

Shamsuddin al-Tabrizi

Meanwhile, Jalaluddin took over his father's old post as teacher in the *madrasa*. He seemed 'destined for a career of modest distinction as an expositor of the faith and the sacred law'. (Arberry, *Discourses of Rumi*, 5) However, on a November's day in 1244, when he was on his way home from the *madrasa*, he was accosted by Shamsuddin al-Tabrizi, an itinerant dervish. Accounts differ as to what exactly happened at this first meeting between the two men, but it was a life-changing experience for Jalaluddin.

The name 'Shams' means 'Sun', and this is what Shams became for Jalaluddin: the dawn rising of a spiritual sun that precipitated an ascent into the higher realms of consciousness. Rumi said of their meeting: 'What I thought of before as God, I met today in a person.' The two men spent days, even months, together in a state of mystical communion, dead to the outer world. But the sudden and total disappearance of Mevlana, their spiritual master, from the life of Konya, its mosque and *madrasa*, aroused resentment among his followers, some of whom threatened Shams.

In the February of 1246, Shams disappeared just as suddenly as he had appeared fifteen months earlier. Perhaps sensing imminent danger he had fled to Damascus. In the spiritual vacuum left by Shams' disappearance, the scholar became a poet, and Mevlana's heightened state of consciousness poured itself forth in ecstatic verse which expressed the mystical love of Lover and Beloved. Some months later news arrived that Shams had been seen in Damascus. A letter was sent asking him to return. Shams refused. More letters followed, and met with the same reply. Eventually Sultan Walad, Mevlana's first son, was sent to bring the errant dervish back.

Shams returned to Konya in May 1247, but it was not long before old resentments resurfaced. One evening in the December of that year, when Mevlana and Shams were together, there was a knock at the door. It was announced that a dervish who had travelled a long distance was asking to see Shams. Shams left the room and was never seen again. Tradition relates that he was attacked and stabbed to death by a gang of assailants led by 'Ala'uddin, Mevlana's second son. Mevlana heard Shams cry out, but by the time he arrived on the scene his body had already been carried away into the night. Some bloodstains on the cobbles in the courtyard were the only clue as to what might have happened to the Sun of Tabriz.

Mevlana was at first inconsolable and even journeyed to Syria in the hope of finding Shams. Yet in looking for Shams in the outside world he found him in the inner. And, as Sultan Walad records, he also found himself:

> He said: Since I am he, what need to seek?
> I am the same as he, his essence speaks!
> Indeed I sought my own self, that is sure,
> Fermenting in the vat, just like the must.
> (Schimmel, *Rumi's World*, 19)

In the earlier verses inspired by Shams, Mevlana did not mention him by name. Then his name began to appear in the middle of the poems. Now, however, Shams was identified as the poet himself. Like a moth drawn into the flame of a candle, Mevlana had been consumed by Love, and had experienced a total passing-away (*fana'*) in the Beloved. For this reason the collection of poems inspired by Shams is usually titled *Divan-i Shams-i Tabriz* ('The Collected Poems of Shams of Tabriz'). Again, Sultan Walad describes his father's spiritual state:

> Never for a moment did he cease from listening to
>   music (sama'), and dancing;
> He had been a mufti: he became a poet;
> He had been an ascetic: he became intoxicated by Love.
> 'Twas not the wine of the grape: the illumined soul
>   drinks only the wine of light.
> (Nicholson, *Rumi: Poet and Mystic*, 20)

Salahuddin Zarkub

Further resentment from Mevlana's followers greeted the prominent position now taken in his life by the goldsmith, Salahuddin Zarkub. Like Mevlana, Salahuddin had been a pupil of Burhanuddin. According to tradition, he was working in the goldsmiths' market in Konya some years later when Mevlana passed by and began to dance in a turning, whirling movement to the sound of the goldsmiths' hammers coming from his workshop. The spiritual relationship Mevlana had formerly enjoyed with Shams continued with

Salahuddin, although perhaps not as extreme, and it was under Salahuddin's name that Mevlana now wrote poetry. The marriage of Mevlana's son, Sultan Walad (now a widower), to Salahuddin's daughter, further strengthened the bond between the two men and they remained close companions until Salahuddin's death in 1258.

Husamuddin Chelebi (Çelebi)

Husamuddin was a young boy when he first met Mevlana and he was still in his teens when he became one of his disciples. He rose to the position of *khalifa* (assistant, or deputy) and became Mevlana's constant companion. It was at his request that Mevlana composed a short 'teaching' poem for the benefit of his disciples. Eighteen verses long, this poem – now known as the Song of the Reed – was destined to become the opening of the *Mathnawi*, for when Mevlana presented it to Husamuddin he said: 'From now on I will recite, and you will write the rest' – 'the rest' extended to six books. It was Mevlana's wish that Husamuddin be his spiritual successor, and in the years immediately following Mevlana's death in 1273 he continued to guide the Mevlevi community according to the ideas and principles of their late master. When Husamuddin died in 1284 he was succeeded by Mevlana's son, Sultan Walad, who was instrumental in founding the Mevleviyyah, the Mevlevi Order of Sufis. In turn Sultan Walad was succeeded by his own son, Arif Chelebi, and this direct line of succession from Mevlana continues to the present day.

The Death of Mevlana

In the autumn of 1273, Mevlana fell ill. The Seljuk sultan, his vizier and other officials came to visit him on his sickbed, and two imperial physicians were in constant attendance. On 17 December Mevlana left this world and was reunited with his Lord, an occasion which is referred to by his followers as his 'wedding night', or 'night of union'. His passing shook Konya, a spiritual equivalent of the earthquakes that had shaken the town earlier that winter. (During the earthquakes he had joked that the earth was hungry, and that she would soon receive 'a fat morsel'.) He was mourned by all its citizens, and, as

Sultan Walad relates, his funeral was attended by people of all religions:

> The people of the city, young and old
> Were all lamenting, crying, sighing loud,
> The villagers as well as Turks and Greeks,
> They tore their shirts from grief for this great man.
> 'He was our Jesus!' – thus the Christians spoke.
> 'He was our Moses!' said the Jews of him . . .
> (Schimmel, *Rumi's World*, 31)

In the centuries following Mevlana's death his tomb has been visited by people from all walks of life, from humble pilgrims to heads of state, and the adjoining *dergah* (convent) of the Mevlevi Order received numerous endowments. During the reign of Suleyman the Magnificent (1520–66), the *semahane* (a ceremonial hall where the *sema* or 'whirling' was done) was built adjoining Mevlana's mausoleum, which was also the burial place of his father, and of his immediate successors. Cells for the dervishes were added under later rulers and fresh endowments led to the founding of new *dergahs* throughout Anatolia and further afield. In 1925, following Ataturk's ban on Sufi Orders in Turkey, the mausoleum and its surrounding complex of buildings were turned into a museum. With its dervish cells, large kitchen, and adjoining *semahane*, the museum gives an idea of the training undertaken by those who wished to be initiated into a Sufi Order.

The Writings of Rumi

Rumi's principal works were written in Persian, and although they have been translated into many languages they are usually referred to by their Persian names: the *Divan-i Shams-i Tabriz*, the *Fihi ma fihi*, and the *Mathnawi*. In these works Rumi brings together the outer and inner worlds in a vast panoply of exoteric and esoteric commentary, not only on the Qur'an, the *ahadith* (the Prophetic Traditions), traditional stories (e.g. Layla and Majnun) and the lives of the Sufi saints who preceded him, but also on Sufi teachings and the Sufi Path. Until quite recently the most widely available translations in English were the work of Oriental scholars, in particular Professor Reynold A. Nicholson and his pupil A. J. Arberry, but a wider public interest was aroused in 1976 by the UNESCO-sponsored celebrations to commemorate the 700-year anniversary of Mevlana's 'night of union'. Books on Mevlana and the Mevlevi path by Annemarie Schimmel and others were published in the late 1970s and, in the early 1980s, American writers such as Kabir Helminski and Coleman Barks (writing on his own or in collaboration with John Moyne) published modern English renderings of excerpts from Rumi's writings. Since then, many more books have been published about Mevlana, his life, his teachings and writings, and books of his poetry have entered the bestseller lists. For some people, he has become synonymous with Sufism itself. (On a recent visit to nearby Glastonbury I found that the 'Sufism' section in one of the New Age bookshops consisted solely of books by or about Rumi.)

Divan-i Shams-i Tabriz

Also known as the *Divan-i Kabir*, this collection of lyrical poetry written by Rumi under the name of Shamsuddin of Tabriz comprises some 2,500 odes and is an impassioned celebration of the Divine Unity – or, perhaps more specifically, of Love. Not to be confused with sentimental or emotional love (which are but pale reflections of it), the Love of which Rumi speaks is the glue that binds the Divine Unity together. For him, Shamsuddin of Tabriz was the embodiment of Love. Or to quote Rumi's own words again: 'What I thought of before as God, I met today in a person.'

In binding us to the Source of our being, Love has the power to heal our sense of separation from the Divine Unity. It is also our means of escape from the twin 'prisons' of our physical body and the material world:

> From the moment you came into the world of being,
> A ladder was placed before you that you might escape.
> (Nicholson, *Selected Poems From the Divani Shamsi Tabriz*, XII)

In the following selection from the *Divan*, the poet expresses the essential nonduality of the Divine Unity within which 'thou' and 'I' are not two.

Happy the moment when we are seated in the palace, thou and I,
With two forms and with two figures but with one soul, thou and I.
The colours of the grove and the voices of the birds will bestow immortality
At the time when we shall come into the garden, thou and I.
The stars of Heaven will come to gaze upon us:
We shall show them the moon herself, thou and I.
Thou and I, individuals no more, shall be mingled in ecstasy,
Joyful and secure from foolish babble, thou and I.
All the bright-plumed birds of Heaven will devour their hearts with envy
In the place where we shall laugh in such a fashion, thou and I.
This is the greatest wonder, that thou and I, sitting here in the same nook,
Are at this moment both in 'Iraq and Khorasan, thou and I.
(*Selected Poems From the Divani Shamsi Tabriz*, XXXVIII)

It happened that we made a journey without 'we';
There our heart blossomed without 'we'
That Full-Moon which was hiding from us
Put Its Face to our face without 'we'.
Without dying in grief for the Beloved,
We were reborn in His grief, without 'we'
We are always intoxicated without wine;
We are always happy without 'we'.
Don't remember us as 'we';
We are our own remembrance, without 'we'.
We are happy together, proclaiming
'Oh, we shall always be without "we".'
All doors were closed to us;
And then the path of Truth
Opened without 'we'.
. . . We have passed beyond right and wrong,
Beyond both prayer and the sins of existence, without 'we'.
(*Selected Poems From the Divani Shamsi Tabriz*)

When my bier moveth on the day of death,
Think not my heart is in this world.
Do not weep for me and cry 'Woe, woe!'
Thou wilt fall in the devil's snare: that is woe.
When thou seest my hearse, cry not 'Parted, parted!'
Union and meeting are mine in that hour.
If thou commit me to the grave, say not 'Farewell, farewell!'
For the grave is a curtain hiding the communion of Paradise.
After beholding descent, consider resurrection;
Why should setting be injurious to the sun and moon?
To thee it seems a setting, but 'tis a rising;
Tho' the vault seems a prison, 'tis the release of the soul.
What seed went down into the earth but it grew?
Why this doubt of thine as regards the seed of man?
(Selected *Poems From the Divani Shamsi Tabriz*, XXIV)

Fihi ma fihi

The title of Professor Arberry's translation of this prose work is *Discourses of Rumi*, but the original Persian title translates literally as 'In it what is in it', which can be further rendered as 'You get out of it what is in it for you', or 'How you understand this will depend upon your level of understanding'. The title reminds us that what we see in the world outside ourselves is really only ever a reflection of ourselves, our opinions, our concepts, our beliefs, and so on; things that limit our capacity for understanding. What we find in a work such as the *Fihi ma fihi* – or for that matter in any inspired literary, theatrical, musical, or visual work – depends upon our level of understanding, or, to put this another way, on our capacity for *hearing* what is being communicated to us. To hear what is really being communicated to us we need to put aside our opinions and prejudices, and at the same time block our ears to the stream of mental chatter that runs incessantly through our minds. Some schools of thought maintain that we need to read a thing at least three times if we are to begin to understand it, because the more we focus our attention on what we are studying the more we free ourselves from the hold that superficial distractions normally exercise over us.

It is generally accepted that the *Discourses* were written down by a scribe while the discourse or conversation was taking place and were possibly corrected later by Rumi himself. Among the subjects he discourses on are the outer and inner worlds, duality and nonduality, the Sufi path to enlightenment and the relationship between the pupil and his/her spiritual mentor. The discourses themselves are enlivened with anecdotes and stories, and in many instances they also incorporate rudimentary lessons in human and spiritual psychology. It is hoped that the following adapted extracts will give the reader a taste of the style and content of the *Discourses*.

The Fourth Discourse

The discourse opens with an unnamed person casually remarking, 'I have forgotten to do something.' From this simple beginning Rumi builds a discourse to remind us that there is one thing which must never be forgotten: we came into this world for a specific purpose, for a particular task that can only be performed by human beings. If we fulfil this purpose, we eradicate 'sin' and 'folly' from our lives; if we do not, we will have done nothing with our lives.

We might say to ourselves, 'Even if I do not perform the task for which I was brought into the world, I have done a lot of other things.' Yet we were not brought into the world to perform these other tasks. Rumi likens it to acquiring a priceless sword of the kind found only in royal treasure houses and turning it into a butcher's knife for cutting up offal, saying, 'I am not letting this sword remain idle, I am putting it to good use.' Or it is like taking a bowl made of solid gold and using it to cook turnips when an ounce of the same gold could buy all the cooking pots we could ever need. Or it is like taking an exquisitely crafted dagger of the finest tempered steel and using it as a nail on which to hang a broken gourd, saying to ourselves, 'I am making excellent use of this dagger. By hanging a gourd from it I am not letting it remain idle.' What a ludicrous state of affairs! When the gourd could be hung from a nail of minimal value, where is the sense in hanging it from a dagger valued at thousands of pounds? Rumi reminds us that God has set a great value on us, for he says:

God has bought from the believer their selves
and their possessions against the gift of Paradise.
(Qur'an 9:111)

Or as the poet says:

You are more precious than both heaven and earth:
What can I more? You know not your own worth.
(Sana'i *Hadiqat al-haqiqa*)

Sell not yourself at little price,
Being so precious in God's eyes.
(Rumi)

God says to us, 'I have bought you, your time, your breath, your possessions, your lives. If you dedicate these things to Me, their value is eternal Paradise. This is what I think you are worth.' On the other hand, if we sell ourselves to Hell it is ourselves we will have wronged, just like the man who used the dagger worth thousands of pounds as a nail from which to hang a gourd.

We make the excuse that we are engaged in high-minded projects, but in reality we do the things we do purely out of self-interest, to further our own ends. We ignore the fact that there is more to life than eating and sleeping, that there is another kind of food which gives us sustenance.

The Prophet said, 'I pass the night in the presence of my Lord, He is giving me things to eat and drink.' In this lower world you have forgotten that heavenly food, being occupied with this material sustenance. Night and day you are nourishing your body. Now this body is your horse, and this lower world is its stable. The food of the horse is not the food of the rider; the rider has his own kind of sleeping and eating and taking enjoyment. But because the animal and the bestial have the upper hand over you, you have lagged behind with your horse in the stable for horses and do not dwell in the ranks of the kings and princes of the world eternal. Your heart

is there, but inasmuch as the body has the upper hand you are
subject to the body's rule and have remained its prisoner.
(Arberry, *Discourses of Rumi*, 28-29)

Rumi illustrates this point with an anecdote about Majnun, the man whose love for Layla caused him to lose his rational mind. As long as Majnun was fully conscious when making his way towards Layla's dwelling-place, he drove his camel in that direction. But whenever his mind wandered and filled itself with thoughts of Layla, he forgot about his camel. The camel took advantage of this lapse in concentration to head back to a certain village where it had its offspring. When he came to his senses, Majnun found that he had journeyed for two days in the opposite direction. Things went on like this for three months, until he eventually cried out, 'This camel is the ruin of me!' At which he jumped down from the camel and continued on foot, singing to himself:

> My camel's desire is behind me, and my desire is before:
> She and I are at cross purposes, and agree no more.
> (*Discourses of Rumi*, 29)

The same discourse includes a story about a certain king who entrusted his son's education to a team of learned men. When they had finished with him the son had mastered the sciences of astrology, geomancy and so forth, even though he was dull-witted and stupid.

One day the king decided to give his son a little test. Placing a ring in his clenched fist, he asked: 'What is in my hand?'

'The thing you are holding in your hand is round, yellow, and hollow,' replied the prince.

'You've described the signs correctly, now tell me what the object is.'

'It's a sieve,' answered the prince.

'What?' exclaimed the king. 'You were able to describe the signs correctly, but in spite of all your learning and knowledge you omitted one trivial fact. How can a sieve fit into my closed hand?'

In his explanation of the story Rumi likens the 'great scholars of the age' to the prince, thus reiterating a point frequently made by Sufis: we can acquire a vast wealth of knowledge through conventional study, but this knowledge relates to matters which do not concern us. When it comes to something of real importance, which concerns us directly and which affects us all, namely self-knowledge, the scholar knows nothing. 'He pronounces on the legality or otherwise of every thing, saying, "This is permitted and that is not permitted, this is lawful and that is unlawful." Yet he knows not his own self, whether it is lawful or unlawful, permissible or not permissible, pure or impure.' (*Discourses of Rumi*, 4, 30) This is true for most of us.

Rumi turns our attention to the ring mentioned in the story to make a further point, one which is related to the principles of *fana'* and *baqa'*. The attributes of being circular, yellow, and hollow are not permanent. If the object is put into a furnace, none of the attributes will remain. Purified of its attributes, the object becomes its essential self. The same applies to the descriptive 'signs' attributed by scholars (and ourselves) to any thing – whether object, action, or word. Outward 'signs' have nothing to do with the essence of a thing, for the essence alone continues when the 'signs' are gone. That is how it is with scholars and their 'signs': they hold forth on all manner of things and explain them and since they have no knowledge of essentials, they conclude that the object in the king's hand is a sieve. (*Discourses of Rumi*, 4, 30)

The discourse concludes with an allegorical word of warning about being led astray by fake teachers. Rumi says he is a bird. He is a nightingale. He is a parrot. If people say to him, 'Make a different sound,' he cannot. Since he is true to what he is, he cannot speak otherwise. However, there are people who have learned to sing like the birds. They are not birds themselves; rather, they are the enemy of birds (Lovers) and their fowler (the Beloved). They sing away so that they will be taken for birds. Tell them to sing a different birdsong and they will readily oblige since they are merely imitating the sounds made by others. If the truth be known, the notes they sing are not their own. They were stolen from other people.

Taken as a whole, the discourse is an example of the 'scatter' method of teaching favoured by Sufis. In this method a key point is reiterated several times, each time in an apparently different guise, so that it is presented in a linear form which can be assimilated more easily by the analytical mind. The key point in this discourse is that we need to be on our guard against deluding ourselves, and being deluded by others. As it says in the Qur'an: 'After the Truth what is there save error?' (Qur'an 10:33)

The Sixth Discourse

Towards the end of the above extract from the Fourth Discourse, Rumi commented on our lack of self-knowledge. There are varying degrees of self-knowledge. For instance, there is the spiritual or mystical self-knowledge expressed in the *hadith* 'Whoso knoweth himself knoweth his Lord'. There is also the self-knowledge which concerns itself with understanding why we do the things we do. The Sufis' profound understanding of human psychology is illustrated in the following extract from the Sixth Discourse. Although it was written over 700 years ago, it offers a succinct description of the psychological phenomenon known as 'projection':

> If you perceive a fault in your brother, the fault which you perceive in him is within yourself. The learned man is like a mirror in which you see your own image, for 'The believer is the mirror of his fellow believer.' Get rid of that fault in you, for what distresses you in him distresses you in yourself.
>
> He [Rumi] went on: An elephant was led to a well to drink. Perceiving himself in the water, he shied away. He supposed that he was shying away from another elephant, and did not realise that it was from himself that he shied away.
>
> All evil qualities – oppression, hatred, envy, greed, mercilessness, pride – when they are within yourself, do not pain you. When you perceive them in another, then you shy away and are pained. A man feels no disgust at his own scab and abscess; he will dip his affected hand into the broth and lick his fingers without turning in the least squeamish. But if he sees a tiny abscess or half a scratch on another's hand, he shies away from that man's broth and has no stomach for it whatever. Evil qualities are just like scabs and abscesses; when they are within a man himself he is not pained by

them, but when he perceives them even to a small degree in another he is pained and disgusted.

(Arberry, *Discourses of Rumi*, 35)

The Mathnawi

As mentioned earlier, the *Mathnawi* grew out of a request from Rumi's *khalifa*, Husamuddin Chelebi, for a short 'teaching' poem. The result was the 'Song of the Reed', the opening verses of the *Mathnawi*, Rumi's major work, which was dictated to Husamuddin over many years until Rumi's death. The work, which takes the form of an extended poem, comprises six books, each with a prose introduction, and owes its title to the Persian for 'couplet' or 'distich'. E. H. Whinfield's abridged translation, first published in 1898, is titled *Masnavi-i-Ma'navi* ('Spiritual Couplets'). It was translated into English in its entirety by Professor Nicholson who, in the introduction to the first volume of his translation, remarks that the *Mathnawi* has 25,700 verses, almost as many as the *Iliad* and *Odyssey* together, and about twice as many as Dante's *Divine Comedy*. But the *Mathnawi* itself is much longer than these works since every verse has twenty-two syllables. (*The Mathnawi of Jalaluddin Rumi*, Vol. II, xiii)

The *Mathnawi* is an exceptional work, not only in length but in style and content, for it blends traditional tales, parables, anecdotes and legends about the Sufi saints with stories about the prophets and commentaries on the Traditions (*ahadith*) and on passages from the Qur'an. Sometimes the stories and commentaries flow smoothly into each other, at other times a story is interrupted by another story which is told to illustrate or underline a certain point before the narrator returns to the first story as though we had never left it. All are woven together to create a framework for Rumi's teaching, which, as in his *Fihi ma fihi*, seems to embody two Qur'anic phrases: 'Whichever way you turn, there is the Face of Allah' and 'We belong to Allah, and to Him we return'. (Qur'an 2:115; 2:156) In fact, the Qur'an permeates the *Mathnawi* to such a degree that the fifteenth-century Sufi poet, Jami, actually described it as the Qur'an in the Persian language. As Annemarie Schimmel points out, however, most of the Qur'anic references will escape the non-Muslim Western reader who, unlike his or her Muslim counterpart, has not memorized the entire Qur'an. Nonetheless, there are references to familiar figures from the

Judaeo-Christian tradition who also feature in the Qur'an, such as Noah, Abraham, Joseph, Moses, Solomon and the Queen of Sheba.

The Song of the Reed

The reed had a special significance for Rumi since it served a dual purpose: it furnished the reed-flute (the *ney*) that played the music to which he danced and the reed-pen with which his poetry was written. In both instances, the function of the musician and the poet can itself be likened to that of the reed, for they too are instruments of the self-expression for a spiritual unity. At one point, Rumi says: 'I am the flute, the music is Thine', but then he quickly corrects himself, saying 'No, no. Thou art the flute and the music': he reminds us that within the Divine Unity there is no separation between the musician, the flute, the music, and the breath that gives them life and makes them what they are. Similarly, the poet dictating the *Mathnawi* sees himself as both pen and poem, before reminding us that these two are not separate from the source of their inspiration, for at the end of Book IV Rumi addresses Husamuddin thus: 'the shaping of the poem is from me, and the spirit of it from thee; nay, I spoke in error: truly both this and that are from thee.' (*The Mathnawi of Jalaluddin Rumi*, Vol IV, 482)

As human beings, it seems that we only become aware of the Divine Unity when we awaken to our separation from it. The pain of this awakening is the starting-point for the Song of the Reed. This is my own version (author), based on the translations of E.H. Whinfield and R.A. Nicholson.

> Listen to the reed and its lament,
>> and how it tells a tale of separation:
> 'Ever since I was singled out from the reed-bed,
>> my refrain has moved men and women to tears.
> I want a heart that has been opened by the pain of separation,
>> so that I may share with them the pangs of deep-seated yearning.
> Every one who has been forced to live far from their source
>> longs for the day when they are reunited with it.
> My haunting tune is heard wherever people are gathered together,
>> by the sad at heart and the joyous alike.

Every one interprets my song according to his emotional state;
 yet not one of them searches out the secrets that lie within.
My secrets are not different from the plaintive sound of my lament,
 but they can not be perceived by the physical senses.
The body is not veiled from the soul, nor the soul from the body,
 yet no one has ever seen the soul.'
The sound of the reed is fire, not mere wind or breath;
 and whoever does not have this fire might as well be dead!
It is Love's fire that ignites the reed,
 It is Love's ferment that permeates the wine.
The reed is the companion of broken-hearted lovers;
 its refrain unveils our innermost secrets.
Have you ever seen a poison and an antidote like the reed?
 Have you ever seen a more sympathetic lover?
The reed describes the bloodstained Path of Love,
 and tells stories about the passion of Majnun.
But just as the tongue speaks only to the ear,
 so this particular sense is only for the sense-less.
In our grief the days have become protracted,
 days wherein pain and sorrow go hand-in-hand.
If our time is spent, let it go – it doesn't matter.
 That which remains is Thou, as Thou art!
Anyone but a fish soon has their fill of water;
 anyone who has no daily bread finds the day long.
No one who is 'raw' understands what it is to be 'ripe',
 and so my discourse must be brief.

The following extended extract has been included to illustrate the breadth of the *Mathnawi*'s subject matter and the way Sufi themes flow one into another as Rumi expands his teaching around the unspoken central theme: 'We belong to Allah, and to Him we return'. (Qur'an 2:156) The extract, which is taken from Book IV (verses 1992–2286) (*The Mathnawi of Jalaluddin Rumi*, Vol. IV, 383–398), has been paraphrased and reduced in length. In the original text, each section is prefaced with an explanatory sentence or two. These have been abridged here.

A youth of Hudhayl is appointed commander

We join Rumi's narrative at the point where he tells of the Prophet, on whom be peace, appointing a young man from the Hudhayl tribe to command a force he was sending to fight the unbelievers. Rumi explains that the strength of an army lies in its commander: an army without a leader is like a body without a head. If we are spiritually dead, it is because we have abandoned our leader. Greed and self-centredness have caused us to behave in a headstrong manner and put our selves in charge. We are like the ass that flees from its burden and heads for the mountains. Its master runs after it, calling out: 'Be warned! If you disappear from my sight, wolves will come at you from every direction and kill you. Don't run away from me, for I am your higher self.'

Rumi says that we, too, are like beasts of burden because our lower self predominates, and the dominant quality determines the nature of a thing. The Almighty intended us to behave like a horse (higher self) rather than an ass (lower self), for a horse responds to the command *ta'al* ('come'). Continuing with the equestrian analogy, Rumi says that the Prophet was put in charge of the stableyard for the lower self. Out of compassion, Allah said to him, 'Say, "*ta'alaw* (come ye), [Qur'an 3:57] so that I may train you: I am the trainer".' But each self has its own separate stable, every bird its own cage; and so people respond in different ways to the call *ta'alaw*. Some are deaf to it. Others are frightened by it.

The way we respond to *ta'alaw* is governed by how we hear it with our senses, and our ears have a special function with regard to hearing the Spirit, the Prophetic Traditions and the revealed scripture. No other organ can fulfil that function. So go through the senses one by one, learning the particular function of each. Rumi then reminds us that we have five external organs of sense-perception and five inner organs (the *lataif*). He compares them to ten ranks of worshippers in the standing posture that is adopted when offering up prayers to Allah.

Rumi draws this point to a close by saying that the Divine Word, *ta'alaw*, is a powerful elixir and not to be underestimated. If people turn away from it, it will not be withheld from them. If their lower self currently has them under its spell, they will benefit from the Word later on. '*Ta'alaw, ta'alaw*, Come ye, come ye.' Hearken to Allah's invitation to the Abode of Peace. Come back from your headstrong, self-centred ways. 'Seek a leader, do not desire leadership.'

An objection to the appointment of the young man as commander

Rumi now returns to the appointment of the young man from the tribe of Hudhayl as commander of the army. Motivated by envy a man objected to the appointment of the youthful leader, and Rumi uses this dissent to comment further on humankind's unenlightened state. Our desire for that which is perishable (impermanent) is the cause of our own perishing. Pride keeps us in a state of separation, dead to the spirit. With a touch of irony, he adds: 'It's wonderful that the spirit is in prison, and all the time it has the key of the prison in its hand.'

The heart's yearning for freedom is evidence enough that freedom exists. Our aversion to the world is like our guardian, dragging us along and saying: 'O you who have lost your way, seek out the right path.' The path is there, but it is hidden from view in a secret place. Rumi comments that the discovery of the path involves us in a vain search. In reality our sense of separation is the subtle beginning of our quest for union and the first intimation of what we are searching for.

The man who raised the objection suggested that it would be better to appoint an older, superior man, of whom there were many in the army, to take command. He continued in this vein for some time, with a flow of objections based on the youth's age, immaturity, inexperience, and so on. Rumi observes that we ignore the fact that this sort of conventional wisdom is merely empty babble when placed beside genuine insight. 'Silence is the sea, and speech is like the river. The sea is seeking thee; do not seek the river.' (*The Mathnawi of Jalaluddin Rumi*, Vol. IV, 386)

Conventional wisdom is a substitute for true sight. It is for those who are absent, not for those who live in the present moment. People who attain insight and understanding have no need for conventional wisdom. When you are with your beloved there is no need for letters or people to serve as intermediaries. Once a person reaches (spiritual) maturity, letters and intermediaries are a hindrance.

Rumi now gives some guidance on how to conduct ourselves in the presence of a person of vision, a 'seer'. Firstly, avoid quoting conventional wisdom; to do so will be evidence of our ignorance. In the presence of a seer the best course of action is to remain silent. This is why we received the divine injunction: 'Be ye silent'. If the seer asks us to speak, speak freely, but say little and don't go on at length. If he asks us to speak at length, comply with his request, and speak with the same modesty as before: even as Rumi in writing these verses, complying is with the request of Husamuddin. When he cuts short what he is saying about the Path, Husamuddin uses all sorts of devices to get him to continue.

How Muhammad, on whom be peace, answered the objector

The man, who continued with his objections in the presence of Muhammad, eventually went too far. Muhammad bit his lip, as if to say, 'Enough!' At this point, Rumi passes comment on someone who would behave in this manner towards a man of vision and insight. He is like a person who brings a bag of dried dung, saying: 'Buy this instead of a musk-scented bag.' His stupidity is such that he holds a lump of camel dung under his nose and exclaims: 'What a delightful smell!' He is so deluded that he thinks he can take in a person whose (inner) organ of smell is accustomed to the scent of the celestial rose-garden.

The forbearance of the wise is mistaken for stupidity. Yet the patience of those who are enlightened is like fine wine, gently intoxicating. It is not like worldly wine, which rises quickly to the head and makes people drunk. The intoxication caused by spiritual wine lasts longer than a night of drunkenness. Alluding to an incident from the story of Joseph and Zulaikha, Rumi reminds us that the women of Egypt drank just one glass of spiritual wine – that is, they saw the beauty of Joseph – and were so intoxicated by it that they cut their fingers.

Bayazid says: 'Glory be to Me!'

Rumi continues the theme of spiritual intoxication with an account of an incident involving Bayazid Bistami, one of the most famous of the 'intoxicated' (as opposed to 'sober') Sufis. The incident, which is related in full elsewhere (*see* page 112), occurred when Bayazid, in a state of ecstatic union with the Divine, proclaimed: 'Glory be to Me! How great is My Majesty!' When the ecstatic state was at an end his followers told him what he had said, accusing him of heresy. Bayazid instructed them to take up their knives and kill him the next time he made a similar pronouncement.

Rumi explains that spiritual intoxication overwhelms reason. Their respective lights are comparable to that of the dawning day and a candle. The next time Bayazid went into a state of ecstasy and made a potentially heretical pronouncement, his followers stabbed at him with their knives. Wherever they stabbed him, it was they who received the wound. Why? Whenever a self-existent person engages in combat with a self-less person – that is, in Sufi terminology one who is non-existent – the self-existent one ends up hurting himself. The self-less person has passed away.

Explaining the objector's eloquence

When he found himself in the presence of the Prophet, the objector fell under the influence of his infinite spiritual intoxication, and he too became drunk. Because he was drunk he neglected to show due respect and began to rant. Rumi makes a distinction between spiritual intoxication and intoxication by alcohol. It is true to say that when we are under the influence of either, we are not ourselves. When an intelligent person (a person governed by their higher self) is intoxicated, they conduct themselves in a refined manner. When an evil person (a person governed by their lower self) is intoxicated, their behaviour becomes worse. Since the majority of people are governed by their lower self, wine (alcohol) has been forbidden to everybody.

The Prophet, on whom be peace, explains why he chose the man of Hudhayl

The Prophet told the objector that he was judging the youth according to his external appearance, and yet there are many black-bearded men (young men) who are old in wisdom and many white-bearded men (old men) whose hearts are full of darkness. It is a person's capacity for understanding that makes them mature, not their white hair. Only blindfolded people consider white hair to be a sign of maturity. Because the only evidence they acknowledge is physical, they look for a physical Path.

Those who have escaped from blind imitation see by the light of Allah and see things as they really are. Pure Light goes to the heart of things. Those who see the inner reality see the heart and ignore the outer form. Try to become mature in intelligence and religion, so that you may become, like the Universal

Intelligence, a seer of the inner reality. When Intelligence revealed itself from non-existence, He (Allah) gave it a robe of honour and a thousand names. If the Intelligence were to manifest itself in a visible form, the light of day would seem dark beside it. If foolishness were to manifest itself in a visible form, the darkness of night would seem like a radiant light beside it.

The intelligent person, the half-intelligent person, and the deluded person

Having broached the subject of spiritual intelligence, Rumi describes how it manifests in three different types of people. Spiritually intelligent people have their own light: they are the self-less followers of their (inner) self. Half-intelligent people look on wholly intelligent people as their (spiritual) eye and cling to them for guidance. But the third type, the asses, have not a gram of intelligence. To illustrate how these three types respond to the inner reality and the snares of the world Rumi tells the story of the three fish.

The Three Fish

The story of the three fish is taken from the ancient collection of tales known as the *Fables of Bidpai*, or *Kalila and Dimna* (see page 147). But, as Rumi says, that is only the husk of the story: his telling provides the 'spiritual kernel'. In the preceding passages he has provided the spiritual context. He also supplies a running commentary to the story, thus helping us to arrive at the 'spiritual kernel' as he goes along.

One day some fishermen passed a lake, and seeing that it contained three large fish they hurried off to fetch their nets. But the fish noticed this and their sixth sense told them of the men's intention. The intelligent fish decided that it was time to leave the lake and head for the ocean, even though the journey would be difficult. Having made up his mind, he decided not to discuss it with the other fish lest some of their anticipated reluctance to leave their home rubbed off on him. If you are a traveller, it's best to take counsel with fellow travellers rather than stay-at-homes. True, the *hadith* says, 'Love of one's country is part of the Faith', but beyond the literal interpretation (the outer meaning) there is an inner meaning to the expression 'loving one's country'.

Rumi illustrates this inner meaning with a comment about the prayers which accompany the ablutions.

The inner meaning of the ablutionary prayers

When performing the ritual ablutions, a separate form of prayer is traditionally recited for each part of the body. For example, when water is snuffed up the nose one begs the Almighty for a scent of Paradise so that the scent will lead one to Paradise, just as the scent of the rose leads one to the rose garden. When washing after relieving oneself, one asks to be cleansed: 'O Lord, cleanse me from this. My hand has reached this place and washed it, but my hand is unable to wash my spirit . . . I have washed my skin clean of defilement: do Thou wash this beloved spirit clean of worldly taints.'
(*The Mathnawi of Jalaluddin Rumi*, Vol. IV, 394)

Using the appropriate form of ablutionary prayer

Rumi's lengthy preface to this section relates that there was once a certain person who, when he relieved himself, used to pray, 'O Lord, let me smell the sweet scent of Paradise' instead of 'O Lord, make me one of those who repent much, and make me one of those who purify themselves'. The latter prayer, which is the formula to be said after relieving oneself, he recited when rinsing his nose.

One day someone overheard him praying for the scent of Paradise after relieving himself, and said: 'You have used the correct form of prayer but applied it to the wrong hole. Why recite the nose-prayer when cleaning your backside? One gets the smell of Paradise through the nose. How could the smell of Paradise come from your bottom?' It is good and appropriate to honour the baser things in life. But be careful not to do the opposite, for the opposite is what takes your freedom away. (If we dishonour or degrade the higher things in life, we also diminish ourselves.) The scent of the rose is for the nose; the hole in your backside is not the place for that smell. How could the scent of Paradise come to you from there? If you seek a sweet smell, look for it in the appropriate place. In the same vein, the phrase 'love of country' is correct, but first we need to know what is meant by our 'country'.

So the wise fish left the lake and set off towards the sea. In the same way that a deer pursued by dogs will run until it can run no more, the fish kept going resolutely until it reached the boundless ocean. It suffered much along the way, but ultimately it was swimming towards its salvation. In the meantime the fishermen returned to the lake with their nets. When he saw them, the half-intelligent fish scolded himself for not having followed the example of the wise fish and headed for the sea. 'Still,' he said to himself, 'there's no point in regretting what might have been. We can't undo the past.'

A captive bird gives counsel

One day a small bird which had been cunningly trapped by a hunter addressed its captor, saying: 'Noble master, in your time you have consumed many oxen and sheep, and sacrificed many camels; but as they never satisfied your hunger, neither will I. Let me go, that I may give you three counsels from which you will be able to tell whether I am wise or foolish. I shall give you the first while in your hand, the second from your roof, and the third from a tree. When you have heard all three, you will consider yourself the most fortunate of men. The first counsel is this: "Do not believe the foolish pronouncements of others".'

The bird flew onto the roof of the man's house, and said: 'The second counsel is this: "Do not grieve over the past. When a thing is over and done, have no regrets about it".' The bird continued: 'Concealed in my body is a precious pearl weighing ten dirhems. By rights that pearl was yours, and ensured the future wealth and prosperity of you and your children. It has gone from you because you were not destined to own it, this pearl whose like is nowhere to be found.' At this the man began to bewail his misfortune.

'Did I not say to you: "Do not grieve over the past"?' said the bird. 'So why are you grieving? Either you misunderstood my counsel or you are deaf. And as for the second counsel, did I not say: "Do not be misguided enough to believe things that are patently absurd." O fool, I myself weigh less than three dirhems; how could a pearl weighing ten dirhems be inside me?'

Coming to his senses, the hunter asked the bird for the third counsel. The bird replied: 'Seeing how much you heeded the first two, why should I waste the third on you?' Rumi brings this aside to a close by saying that to give counsel to someone who is both ignorant and fast asleep is like sowing seed on barren soil. He concludes by counselling those who counsel others, saying: 'The tattered garments of folly and ignorance are such that they can not be patched. Don't waste the seeds of wisdom on them.'

How the half-intelligent fish escaped by feigning death

The half-intelligent fish said to himself: 'I've lost a good friend, but it's not the right moment to be thinking of him. I need to attend to my own predicament. I'll pretend to be dead and float belly up in the water, allowing myself to be carried by the current. To die before dying is to be safe from tribulation.' Reminding his audience that the last sentence derives from the *hadith*, 'Die before you die', Rumi continues the story with the half-intelligent fish rolling over on its back so that it floated belly up. One of the fishermen saw it and called out to the others: 'It's a pity, the best fish is dead.'

The half-intelligent fish was heartened to know that his ruse was working. Then one of the fishermen scooped him out of the water and threw him on the ground. Making sure he wasn't seen, the fish rolled over and over until he reached the stream, where he dropped into the water and from there made his way to the ocean.

Meanwhile the foolish fish swam wildly about, up and down the lake, and from side to side, trying desperately to save himself. When the fishermen cast their net into the water he swam right into it. Folly and he were united when he was dropped into a pan to be cooked over a fire. As he began to sizzle he vowed to himself: 'If I escape from this situation, I will not live in a lake. I will make my home nowhere but in the ocean. There I will be forever safe.'

The *Mathnawi* is a very long work – the above extract comprises about 300 of the 25,700 verses – but its essence is summed up in a story told about a meeting between Rumi and Yunus Emre, an Anatolian Sufi of the Bektashi Order. Whereas Rumi's life is fairly well documented, little is known about Yunus. It is clear, however, that the two men came from very different backgrounds: Rumi received a formal education and taught in the *madrasa* in Konya; Yunus was a shepherd who lived a very humble existence. One of the things they had in common was their poetry, yet here again their different backgrounds are evident: Rumi wrote in Persian, Yunus in Turkish. The poetry of both is still popular today, although Yunus is less well known outside his native Turkey.

The story relates that when Jalaluddin Rumi and Yunus Emre met, Yunus was asked what he thought of the *Mathnawi*. He replied: 'It's a little long. I would have written it differently.'

Oh, how so?' asked Rumi.

'I would have written: "I came from eternity, clothed myself with skin and bones and called myself 'Yunus' ".' (Kabir Helminski and Refik Algan *The Drop That Became The Sea* 9)

Whether this anecdote is literally true or not is less important than the potential insight it gives us into the way truly self-less human beings – whatever outer path they follow – experience life on planet Earth. It is so very different from our own.

Shabistari and
The Secret Rose Garden

> *The journey of the pilgrim is two steps and no more:*
> *One is the passing out of selfhood,*
> *And one towards mystical Union with the Friend.*

Sa'd ud Din Mahmud Shabistari – generally known simply as Shabistari – was born c.1250 at Shabistar, near Tabriz in Persia, and died in 1320. Very little is known of his life, except that he was the author of the *Gulshan i Raz* ('The Secret Rose Garden') and two other treatises on Sufism. According to Florence Lederer, the translator, the *Gulshan i Raz* was introduced into Europe in 1700, by two travellers. The work was translated into German and English during the nineteenth century.

When Rumi asked 'Have you ever plucked a rose, from R, O, S, E?' he was mocking those who know the name but have no direct experience of the reality. Something similar may be said of symbols and the reality behind them – especially of the rose, traditional symbol of love and of the heart. The heart blossoms through our direct experience of love for another. Or, if our experience of love is painful, it may wither. A similar principle applies to our spiritual heart, which can be likened to a rose garden that is dedicated to the cultivation of our love for the Beloved. If we journey to the centre of the rose garden we eventually enter the 'secret' rose garden, our innermost heart. Here we pass beyond the duality of 'lover' and 'Beloved' to the realm where there is only Love.

The sense of authenticity, of knowing, that comes from direct experience is expressed in the Sufi saying: 'He who tastes, knows'. It is in this spirit that we may approach Shabistari's *Secret Rose Garden*, the purpose of which is the cultivation of our love for the Beloved.

Shabistari's *Secret Rose Garden* is also an appropriate place to end this introductory book on the Sufis, for many of its themes have been encountered in the preceding pages. The selection of verses is presented here without further comment, except to say that the translation is by Florence Lederer.

III. The Sea and Its Pearls

A Drop of Sea-water

Behold how this drop of sea-water
Has taken so many forms and names;
It has existed as mist, cloud, rain, dew, and mud,
Then plant, animal, and perfect man;
And yet it was a drop of water
From which these things appeared.
Even so this universe of reason, soul, heavens, and bodies,
Was but a drop of water in its beginning and ending.

. . . When a wave strikes it, the world vanishes;
And when the appointed time comes to heaven and stars,
Their being is lost in not being.

Pearls of Knowledge

In the sea of 'Uman, the pearl oysters
Rise to the surface from the lowest depths,
And wait with opened mouths.
Then arises from the sea a mist,
Which falls again in raindrops
Into the mouths of the shells
(At the command of the Truth).
Straightway is each closed as by a hundred bonds,
And the shells sink back again
Into the ocean's depths,
Bearing in their hearts the pearl drops
Which the divers seek and find.

The sea is Being, the shore the body;
The mist, grace, and the rain, knowledge of the Name.
Human wisdom is the diver
Who holds enwrapped in his garment
A hundred pearls;
The soul in a swift lightning's flash
Bears to the listening ear voices and messages
From the shells of knowledge;
Then when the husks are opened,
Behold the royal shimmering pearls!

IV. The Journey

The Traveller

The traveller on the path,
'Tis he who knows from whence he cometh;
Then doth he journey hastily,
Becoming as pure from self as fire from smoke.
Unfolded to him are a series of revelations
From the beginning. Till he is led away
From darkness and sin.
He now retraces stage by stage his steps
Till he reaches his goal in the Perfect.
Thus is the perfect man evolved
From the time he first exists
As inorganic matter,
Next a breath of spirit, and he is living
And from God draws his motive powers.
Next the Truth makes him lord of his will,
As in childhood his discernment of the world unfolds.
And now the world's temptations assail him.

. . . Anger appears and desires of the flesh,
And then avarice, pride, and gluttony;
His nature becomes evil,
Worse than an animal or demon;
Now is he at the lowest point of all,
The point opposite to Unity.

. . . Should he remain fettered in this snare,
He goes further astray than the beasts;
But if there shines a light from the spirit world,
Divinely attractive,
Or if he can find a reflection of proof,
Then will his heart respond in a feeling of kinship
To this Light of the Truth,
And he will turn back and retrace his steps
From whence he came.
To faith assured he has found his way
Through certain proof, or the wonder
And attraction of the Divine.

. . . He throws away his selfhood utterly
And ascends in the steps of the most Pure.

Logic

If God guides you not into the road,
It will not be disclosed by logic.

Logic is a bondage of forms;
A road that is long and hard.
Leave it for a season. Like Moses
Cast away that staff
And enter for awhile 'The Valley of Peace'.

Intermingling

You are plurality transformed into Unity,
And Unity passing into plurality;
This mystery is understood when man
Leaves the part and merges in the Whole.

VII. Divine Inebriation

Tavern-Haunters

The tavern is the abode of lovers,
The place where the bird of the soul nests,
The rest-house that has no existence
In a world that has no form.
The tavern-haunter is desolate in a lonely desert,
Where he sees the world as a mirage.
The desert is limitless and endless,
For no man has seen its beginning or ending.
Though you feverishly wander for a hundred years
You will be always alone.
For the dwellers there are headless and footless,
Neither the faithful nor infidels,
They have renounced both good and evil,
And have cast away name and fame,
From drinking the cup of selflessness;
Without lips or mouth,
And are beyond traditions, visions, and states,
Beyond dreaming of secret rooms, of lights and miracles

They are lying drunken through the smell of the wine-dregs,
And have given as ransom
Pilgrim's staff and cruse,
Dentifrice and rosary.

Sometimes rising to the world of bliss,
With necks exalted as racers,
Or with blackened faces turned to the wall,
Sometimes with reddened faces tied to the stake.

Now in the mystic dance of joy in the Beloved,
Losing head and foot like the revolving heavens.
In every strain which they hear from the minstrel
Comes to them rapture from the unseen world.

For within the mere words and sounds
Of the mystic song
Lies a precious mystery.
From drinking one cup of the pure wine,
From sweeping the dust of the dung-hills from their souls,
From grasping the skirts of drunkards,
They have become Sufis.

From **Wine, Torch, and Beauty**

Drink this wine and, dying to self,
You will be freed from the spell of self.
Then will your being, as a drop,
Fall into the ocean of the Eternal.

Intoxication

What is pure wine?
It is self-purification.
What sweetness! what inebriation! what blissful ecstasy!
Oh! happy the moment when ourselves we quit,
When fallen in the dust, drunken and amazed,
In utter poverty we shall be rich and free.
Of what use then will be paradise and houris?
For no alien can find entrance to that mystic room.

I know not what will happen after
I have seen this vision and imbibed this cup,
But after all intoxication comes headache,
Anguish drowns my soul remembering this!

VIII. Reason and Free-will

Reason

Let reason go. For his light
Burns reason up from head to foot.

If you wish to see that Face,
Seek another eye. The philosopher
With his two eyes sees double,
So he is unable to see the unity of the Truth.

As his light burns up the angels,
Even so does it consume reason.
As the light of our eyes to the sun,
So is the light of reason to the Light of Lights.

Knowledge

Learning is only the outer wrapping of the letter;
The dry husk that covers the nut,
Not the kernel concealed within;
Yet must the husk exit
To ripen the kernel.
So from learning comes the sweet knowledge of Faith.

Oh! soul of my brother, hearken,
Strive to gain knowledge of faith,
For the 'knower' in both worlds
Has a high place.
Knowledge loves not this world of form
Which is void of Reality.

Begin to till your field
For next year's harvest.
Knowledge is your heritage,
Be adorned with the principle of all virtues.

The Blindness of Reason

As the man blind from birth
Believes not nor understands
Your description of colours,
Even if you showed him proofs for a century,
So blind reason cannot see the future state.
But beyond reason man has a certain knowledge
Which God has placed in his soul and body
Whereby he perceives hidden mysteries.
And like the fire in flint and steel
When these are struck together,
The two worlds for him are lit up in a flash.

Free-Will

You say, 'I myself have Free-will,
For my body is the horse and my soul the rider,
The reigns of the body are in the hands of the soul,
The entire direction is given to me.'

Oh! foolish one, these are falsehoods and delusions
That come from an illusory existence.

As your essence is nothingness,
How can you have Free-will?
Seeing that your being is one with not-being,
Whence comes this Free-will of yours?

Imagination distributes actions
As in a play or a farce,
For when your actions were planned,
Before your existence,
You were created for a certain purpose,
By the desire of the Truth.
Therefore is a man predestined, before his existence,
To certain appointed work.
. . . (Oh, wondrous ways of Thine, without how or why!)

The honour of man consists of slavery,
In having no share of Free-will.

Of himself man has nothing,
Yet of good and evil God asks him,
Man has no choice, he is under control.
Oh! poor soul, he seems free, yet he is a slave.

Give yourself up to the Truth,
For you are helpless in his grasp;
Freedom from self you will find in the All,
And, O Dervish! in the Truth you will find riches.

IX. Man: his capabilities and his destiny

'I' and 'You'

'I' and 'you' are but the lattices,
In the niches of a lamp,
Through which the One Light shines.

'I' and 'you' are the veil
Between heaven and earth;
Lift this veil and you will see
No longer the bond of sects and creeds.

When 'I' and 'you' do not exist,
What is mosque, what is synagogue?
What is the Temple of Fire?

The Written Faith

Read the writing on your heart,
And you will understand whatever you desire,
For on the day He kneaded the clay,
He wrote on your heart, by grace, the faith.

XI. The Self

Transcend Self

Rise above time and space,
Pass by the world, and be to yourself your own world.

Selflessness

In the empty heart, void of self
Can be heard the echoing cry,
'I am the Truth.'
Thus is man one with the Eternal,
Travelling, travel and traveller have become one.

Afterword

It is almost seven hundred years since Shabistari wrote *The Secret Rose Garden*, and almost nine hundred since the death of Imam Ghazali, whose writings brought Part One of this book to a close. Although our brief historical survey included the names of a number of Sufi shaykhs and masters who have been active in the West during the late twentieth and early twenty-first centuries, the reader may be wondering why little or no mention has been made of the writings of the Sufis from the intervening centuries.

One reason is that most of the writings in the present book date from a time when it was considered necessary to demonstrate to the orthodox religious authorities that the Sufis and their teachings were neither heretical nor blasphemous. The best vehicle for this was an explanatory treatise setting out the esoteric teachings of the Sufis in an exoteric language that could be understood by the uninitiated. Once the numerous Sufi treatises had fulfilled this purpose and Sufism had been acknowledged as the mystical heart of Islam, there was no longer a need to produce writings to demonstrate the point.

A second reason is that the Sufi Path has for the most part been an initiatory path (the *tariqah*) whose teachings have been passed on orally down the centuries – from the thirteenth century onwards via the Sufi Orders and the chain of transmission (*silsilah*) from shaykh to shaykh. In some instances a shaykh may have committed his teaching to the written word, but this has often been solely for use within the Order itself and not for wider publication. Only when such writings have been translated into one or other of the major European languages have they become available to a wider Western audience. That said, the expansion of Sufi Orders in the West during the twentieth and twenty-first centuries has given many thousands of Westerners direct access to Sufi teachings, both oral and written.

Those readers wishing to learn more about the Sufis and Sufism are reminded that there are at least two schools of thought: one insists that there can be no Sufism without Islam and the other holds that the timeless truths of the Sufis are universal in nature and cannot therefore be confined to one particular religion. The bibliography at the back of this book includes a number of titles that can be recommended for those who wish to read further. General introductions that go into greater depth in some areas not covered by the present book are Martin Lings' *What is Sufism?*, Idries Shah's *The Sufis* and *The Way of the Sufi* and Dr H. J. Witteveen's *Universal Sufism*. One area that has regrettably been given less attention in this book than I would have wished is the important role of women in Sufism, and to rectify this omission I recommend Camille Adams Helminski's *Women of Sufism* and Dr. Javad Nurbaqsh's *Sufi Women*. The writings of contemporary Sufi shaykhs are becoming more widely available and the reader should have no difficulty finding books on or about Jalaluddin Rumi. A visit to a bookshop specialising in esoteric literature will provide a hands-on opportunity to browse through some of the material available. Alternatively one can browse the websites of the various Internet booksellers, or contact publishers such as Threshold Books (Putney, Vermont), Shambhala (Boston and London), Fons Vitae (Louisville, Kentucky) or The Islamic Texts Society (Cambridge).

Things are a little more complex for those readers who may wish to make direct contact with the Sufis or a Sufi Order. Sufis do not advertise their presence in the way that the practitioners of other religious or spiritual traditions might. Self-promotion often arises from the ego's need to draw attention to itself and so there is little or no place for it among the Sufis. In countries where Islam is the dominant religion this presents no problem. In the West, however, this deliberately low profile approach has given rise to the misconception that the Sufis are a secretive or exclusive (even élitist) organization. Such misconceptions arise from our tendency to try to force-fit things into our current level of understanding rather than acknowledge that there are some things which it simply cannot accommodate. (This particular tendency is illustrated in the story about Mulla Nasrudin which began this book.) The Internet has made things a little easier, however, thanks to its powerful search engines.

Sufis themselves often make the point that a Sufi school or Order may arise in a particular place at a particular time in order to meet the spiritual needs created by a particular set of circumstances. Once those needs have been met, the school or Order will either disappear or change its outer form in response to the evolving spiritual needs of the group or community involved. Sufis also comment on our human tendency to be attracted by celebrity – that is, we are drawn towards the high-profile celebrity guru or teacher. The point is often made that if we find ourselves in a physically life-threatening situation, we accept help from whoever is competent and qualified to give it. We do not wait until a celebrity life-saver comes along. Yet where our spiritual well-being is concerned, our desire to be associated with the famous can mean that (to our own detriment) we ignore the humble teacher living a few doors away from us. This is particularly true of the Sufis, many of whom remain invisible to normal eyes. It is to these that Abu Sai'id referred when he said: 'The true saint goes in and out amongst the people and eats and sleeps with them and buys and sells in the market and takes part in social intercourse, and never forgets God for a single moment.'

Appendices

Appendix One

The Most Beautiful Names

The Most Beautiful Names correspond to God's attributes or qualities and one of the goals of the Sufi path is for His attributes to replace our own. A *hadith* instructs us to 'Pattern yourselves on God's characteristics', while another explains this more fully: 'Verily, God has ninety-nine characteristics; whosoever patterns himself on one of them, enters Paradise.' One of the ways to immerse oneself in a particular quality is through recitation, for which a rosary (*tasbih*) with ninety-nine beads is used to keep track of the number of repetitions. In the Sufi practice known as *wazifah*, the shaykh prescribes a particular name for a disciple and the number of times the name is to be repeated. This practice should only be performed under the guidance of an experienced Sufi shaykh.

Lists of the Ninety-Nine Names often vary in their translation of individual qualities into English. The following list includes several standard variations with a view to giving a more comprehensive 'taste' of the quality associated with a particular Name.

1. Ar-Rahman	The Compassionate; The Beneficent; The Gracious; The Infinitely Good; The All Merciful.

2. Ar-Rahim	The Merciful; The All-Beneficent.
3. Al-Malik	The King; The Sovereign Lord; The Absolute Ruler.
4. Al-Quddus	The Holy; The Pure One.
5. As-Salam	The Peace; The Flawless; The Saviour.
6. Al-Mu'min	The Faithful; The One with Faith; The Inspirer of Faith; The Keeper of Faith; The Bestower of Security.
7. Al-Muhaymin	The Protector; The Guardian.
8. Al-'Aziz	The Mighty; The Victorious; The Eminent.
9. Al-Jabbar	The Repairer; The Restorer; The Compeller.
10. Al-Mutakabbir	The Majestic; The Greatest; The Superb; The Proud; The Imperious.
11. Al-Khaliq	The Creator.
12. Al-Bari'	The Producer; The Maker of Order; The Maker-out-of-Naught.
13. Al-Musawwir	The Fashioner; The Shaper of Beauty; He who gives form.
14. Al-Ghaffar	The Forgiver; The Forgiving; He who is full of forgiveness.
15. Al-Qahhar	The Almighty; The Dominator; The Conquering; The Subduer; The Crusher.

16. Al-Wahhab	The Bestower; The Giver of All.
17. Ar-Razzaq	The Provider; The Sustainer.
18. Al-Fattah	The Opener; The Opener of the inward eye; The Reliever; The Judge.
19. Al-'Alim	The Knower; The Knower of All; The All-Knowing; The Omniscient.
20. Al-Qabid	The Withholder; The Restrainer; The Constrictor; The Straitener; The Contracter; He who contracts.
21. Al-Basit	The Reliever; The Spreader; The Enlarger; The Extender; The Expander; He who expands; The Munificent.
22. Al-Khafid	The Abaser; The Humbler.
23. Ar-Rafi'	The Exalter.
24. Al-Mu'izz	The Enhancer; The Strengthener; The Bestower of Honours; The Honourer.
25. Al-Mudhill	The Abaser; He who humbles; The Humiliator; The Dishonourer.
26. As-Sami'	The Hearer; The Hearer of All; The All-Hearing.
27. Al-Basir	The Perceiver; The Seer; The Seer of All; The All-Seeing.

28. Al-Hakam	The Arbitrator; The Decider; The Judge.
29. Al-'Adl	The Just.
30. Al-Latif	The Subtle One; The Subtle; The Benign; The Gracious; The Benevolent.
31. Al-Khabir	The Aware; The All-Aware; The Totally Aware; He who is aware of everything.
32. Al-Halim	The Mild; The Gentle; The Forbearing; The Clement; The Indulgent.
33. Al-'Azim	The Magnificent; The Tremendous; The Immense; The Mighty.
34. Al-Ghafur	The Forgiver and Hider of Faults; The All-Forgiving.
35. Ash-Shakur	The Grateful; The Repayer of Good; The Rewarder of Thankfulness.
36. Al-'Ali	The Sublime; The Most High; The Highest.
37. Al-Kabir	The Great; The Greatest.
38. Al-Hafiz	The Protector; The Guardian; The All-Preserver.
39. Al-Muqit	The Sustainer; The Strengthener; The Giver of Strength; The Nourisher; The Feeder.

40. Al-Hasib	The Reckoner; The Accounter; The All-Calculating.
41. Al-Jalil	The Majestic; The Mighty.
42. Al-Karim	The Generous; The Bountiful.
43. Ar-Raqib	The Watcher; The Watchful One; The All-Observant.
44. Al-Mujib	The Responsive; The Responder (to Prayer); The Answerer of prayers; The Hearkener (to prayer).
45. Al-Wasi'	The Comprehensive; The Vast; The All-Comprehending; The All-Embracing; The All-Containing; The Englober.
46. Al-Hakim	The Wise; The Perfectly Wise.
47. Al-Wadud	The Loving; The Loving One; The Lovingkind.
48. Al-Majid	The Majestic One; The Glorious; The All-Glorious.
49. Al-Ba'ith	The Sender; The Raiser (from death); The Raiser of the dead; The Resurrector.
50. Ash-Shahid	The Witness; The Universal Witness.
51. Al-Haqq	The Truth.
52. Al-Wakil	The Reliable; The Trustee; The Guardian; The Advocate; The Representative.

53. Al-Qawi	The Strong; The Possessor of All Strength.
54. Al-Matin	The Steady; The Steadfast; The Firm; The Forceful One.
55. Al-Wali	The Helper; The Patron; The Friend; The Protecting Friend; The Friend and Protector.
56. Al-Hamid	The Laudable; The Praiseworthy; The Praised; The Praised One.
57. Al-Muhsi	The Appraiser; The Counter; The Accountant; The Knower of each separate thing.
58. Al-Mubdi	The Cause; The Beginner; The Originator; The Producer.
59. Al-Mu'id	The Restorer; The Bringer-back; The Reproducer.
60. Al-Muhyi	The Quickener; The Life-Giver; The Giver of Life.
61. Al-Mumit	The Destroyer; The Slayer; The Causer of Death; The Death-Giver; The Taker of Life.
62. Al-Hayy	The Alive; The Living; The Ever-Living; The Everliving One.
63. Al-Qayyum	The Self-Subsistent; The Self-Subsisting; The Self-Existing; The Self-Existing One; The All-Sustaining; The Eternal.

64. Al-Wajid   The Finder; The Resourceful; The Illustrious;
                      The Noble.

65. Al-Majid   The Magnificent; The Glorious; The Noble.

66. Al-Wahid   The Unique; The Only One.

67. Al-Ahad   The One.

68. As-Samad   The Satisfier of all Needs;
                      He who has absolute plenitude;
                      The Eternal Support of Creation;
                      The Eternal.

69. Al-Qadir   The Capable; The Able; The All-Powerful.

70. Al-Muqtadir   The Prevailing; The Powerful;
                      The Creator of All Power;
                      The All-Determiner; The Dominant.

71. Al-Muqaddim   The Expediter; The Promoter;
                      The Bringer-Forward; He who brings forward.

72. Al-Mu'akhkir   The Retarder; The Delayer; The Deferrer;
                      The Postponer.

73. Al-Awwal   The First.

74. Al-Akhir   The Last.

75. Az-Zahir   The Outward; The Manifest;
                      The Manifest One.

76. Al-Batin   The Inward; The Hidden; The Hidden One.

77. Al-Wali	The Ruler; The Governor.
78. Al-Muta'ali	The Exalted; The High Exalted; The Sublime; The Transcendent; The Supreme One.
79. Al-Barr	The Doer of Good; The Benefactor; The Righteous.
80. At-Tawwib	The Relenting; The Ever-relenting; The Guide to Repentance; He who makes repentance easy; The Accepter of Repentance.
81. Al-Muntaqim	The Avenger.
82. Al-'Afu	The Mild; The Effacer of sins; The Pardoner; The Forgiver; The Indulgent.
83. Ar-Ra'uf	The Clement; The Full of Pity; The All-Pitying; The Compassionate; The Pardoner.
84. Malik al-Mulk	The Ruler of the Kingdom; The King of Absolute Sovereignty; The Owner of Sovereignty; The Owner of All.
85. Dhul-Jalali Wal-Ikram	The Lord of Majesty and Generosity; The Lord of Majesty and Bounty.
86. Al-Muqsit	The Equitable; The Requiter.
87. Al-Jami'	The Gatherer; The Collector; The Assembler; The Uniter.

88. Al-Ghani	The Rich; The Rich One; The Self-Sufficient; The Independent.
89. Al-Mugni	The Enricher.
90. Al-Mani'	The Withholder; The Preventer; The Preventer of Harm; The Shielder; The Protector.
91. Ad-Dar	The Punisher; The Distresser; The Creator of the Harmful.
92. An-Nafi'	The Propitious; The Profiter; The Benefactor; He who benefits; The Creator of Good.
93. An-Nur	The Light.
94. Al-Hadi	The Guide
95. Al-Badi'	The Incomparable; The Inventor; The Originator; The Absolute Cause.
96. Al-Baqi	The Enduring; The Permanent; The Everlasting; The Everlasting One.
97. Al-Warith	The Heir; The Inheritor; The Inheritor of All.
98. Ar-Rashid	The Director; The Rightly Guided; The Right in Guidance; The Guide to the Right Path; The Righteous Teacher.
99. As-Sabur	The Patient; The Patient One.

Appendix Two

Glossary of Sufi terminology

'abd   servant, slave. In contrast to the filial (Father-child) relationship of
            Christianity, in Islam the relationship between God and human
            beings is viewed as being that of Lord and servant/slave – a
            reminder that *islam* entails the surrender of our whole being to
            the Divine Will. (*see* Ibrahim ibn Adham and the servant/slave,
            page 98)

baqa'   from the same root as *al-Baqi,* one of the Ninety-Nine Names,
            baqa' refers to the Divine Attribute of Everlastingness or
            Continuance. It is the opposite of the term *fana'*, which means
            'passing away'. Both terms are met in a verse in the Qur'an:
            'Everything upon the earth shall pass away; but the Face of the
            Lord shall remain forever . . .' (Qur'an 55:26–27) That which
            passes away is impermanent, transient. That which remains is
            permanent, enduring. The principle of 'passing away' or 'dying to
            self' (*fana'*) is also implied in the *hadith* 'Die before you die'.
            When the Sufi attains the stage of *fana'* in the Sufi Path and leaves
            his/her self behind, that which remains is the Divine Self.

barakah   blessing, grace, spiritual influence.

barzakh   isthmus. The heart is the isthmus (or bridge) between the two worlds.

basmalah   the opening phrase of the Qur'an, and the opening phrase of every surah except the ninth: *Bismi Llah ir-Rahman ir-Rahim* (In the Name of Allah, the Beneficent, the Merciful). As a consecrational formula it is repeated before carrying out many daily duties or functions.

dervish   see *faqir*.

dhikr   recollection, remembrance. Used in the sense of remembering God (as opposed to forgetting Him, which is *ghaflah*), for as Allah says in the Qur'an: 'Remember Me. I will remember you.' (Qur'an 2:152) The practice of *dhikr*, or more specifically *dhikru 'llah*, refers to the invocation of one of the Divine Names, or certain other formulae, such as the *shahadah*.

divan   a collection of poetry, as in Jalaluddin Rumi's *Divan-i Shams-i Tabriz* ('The Collected Poems of Shams of Tabriz').

fana'   passing-away, annihilation (of the self). The final stage of *fana'* is *fana' al-fana'* (the passing-away of passing-away), when one is no longer conscious of having attained *fana'*. (see also *baqa'*)

faqir   a poor man. A term used to denote a follower of the Sufi Path. A *faqir* is spiritually 'poor' – that is, he/she seeks to relinquish 'the self' and its associated 'riches'. The Persian for *faqir* is *darwish* and from these two words come the English '*fakir*' and '*dervish*'.

fiqh   Islamic jurisprudence.

fitrah   our primordial or uncorrupted nature, before it became veiled by the desires and emotional reactions of our lower self, by mental concepts and prejudices and by the effects of social and cultural conditioning.

ghaflah forgetfulness, ignorance. The opposite of *dhikr*, which is the conscious recollection or remembrance of God.

ghazal a short poem of between ten and fifteen verses, used primarily for love poetry.

hal (plur. *ahwal*) spiritual state. (see *also* states and stations)

hadith (plur. *ahadith*) saying or statement of the Prophet Muhammad. A *hadith qudsi* is a 'Divine Saying', in which Allah speaks through the mouth of the Prophet.

haqiqah inner reality; from the same root as *al-haqq*, meaning 'the Truth' or 'the Real'. (see also *shari'ah* and *tariqah*)

ihsan virtue, spiritual life. One of the three basic principles of Islam, the other two being *iman* and *islam*.

iman faith. One of the three basic principles of Islam, the other two being *islam* and *ihsan*.

insan al-kamil 'Perfect' or 'Universal' Man. A term used to denote a fully realized human being.

islam submission to the Divine Will. One of the three basic principles of Islam, the other two being *iman* and *ihsan*.

khanaqah see *zawiyah*.

Khidr the 'Green One'. A mysterious figure who met Moses near the fountain of life; their meeting and journey together are described in the Qur'an (18:64–82). Although he is unnamed in the Qur'an, the name al-Khidr has been passed down by oral tradition. He is immortal and appears at crucial times to those in need of guidance.

lataif   (sing. *latifah*) the five organs of subtle or inner perception. Their names, locations and associated colours are: *qalb* (mind or heart), left side of chest, yellow; *ruh* (spirit), right side of chest, red; *sirr* (inner consciousness), solar plexus, white; *khafi* (hidden depth or intuition), forehead, black; *akhfa* (most hidden depth or deep consciousness), centre of chest, green. The *lataif* are not to be confused with the *chakras* or energy centres of Eastern tradition.

maqam   (plur. *maqamat*) spiritual station. (*see also* states and stations)

mathnawi   rhyming couplet. A poetic form used by Attar, Rumi and others.

nafs   (plur. *nufus*) variously defined as soul, mind, self or ego. The *nafs* is frequently described as having seven levels or stages: the Commanding Self; the Accusing or Reproachful Self; the Inspired Self; the Tranquil or Certain Self; the Satisfied or Contented Self; the Harmonious or Satisfying Self; the Fulfilled or Purified and Completed Self. The passage through these seven stages constitutes a path of transformation.

ruba'i   a quatrain.

shari'ah   the sacred Law of Islam; 'outer reality' as opposed to the 'inner reality' of *haqiqah*.

shaykh   a Sufi spiritual master, not to be confused with a shaykh/sheikh who is the leader of a tribe or village.

shirk   polytheism, associationism; the opposite of *tawhid*.

Glossary of Sufi Terminology

silsilah   the chain or line of succession by which a Sufi Order (*tariqah*) traces its descent from the Prophet Muhammad via an unbroken initiatic lineage passed from *shaykh* to *shaykh*.

states and stations spiritual states (*ahwal*) (e.g. love, certainty, nearness to God, ecstasy) are gifts 'from above' and are transient; spiritual stations (*maqamat*) (e.g. conversion, renunciation, poverty) are acquired through individual effort and are permanent.

Sufi Path   the number of stages on the Sufi Path varies according to the particular commentator or source. Writing in 1046, Qushairi outlined forty-five stages in his *Risala*; others talk of only two – the first is to step out of the self, the second is to step into union with God. In Attar's *Conference of the Birds*, the Path has seven stages or 'valleys'.

tariqah   the spiritual Path leading from *shari'ah to haqiqah*. The word *tariqah* also denotes a Sufi Order or brotherhood, such as the Qadiriyyah, Naqshbandiyyah or Mevleviyyah.

tasawwuf   Sufism, Islamic mysticism.

tawhid   affirmation of the Divine Unity; the opposite of *ghaflah*.

'ulama'   the religious authorities of Islam (scholars, jurists, etc.) as opposed to the spiritual authorities who are the Sufi *shaykhs*.

wali   saint, or friend of God.

zawiyah   (literally 'a corner') Sufi meeting-place (Persian *khanaqah*; Turkish *tekke*).

Bibliography

Ad-Darqawi, Shaykh al-'Arabi. *Letters of a Sufi Master*, tr. Titus Burckhardt 1969; Fons Vitae, Louisville, KY 1998

Affifi, A. E. *The Mystical Philosophy of Muhyid Din-Ibnul Arabi* Cambridge, 1939

Al-Ghazali. *The Alchemy of Happiness*, tr. C. Field Ashraf Press, Lahore n.d.

Al-Ghazali. *The Confession of Al-Ghazzali*, tr. C. Field Ashraf Press, Lahore n.d.

Al-Ghazali. *The Ninety-Nine Beautiful Names of God*, tr. David Burrell and Nazih Daher Islamic Texts Society, Cambridge 1995

Amuli, Sayyid Haydar. *Inner Secrets of the Path*, tr. Assadulah ad-Dhaakir Yate Element Books, Shaftesbury 1989

Arasteh, A. Reza. *Growth to Selfhood* Routledge & Kegan Paul, London 1980

Arberry, A. J. *Discourses of Rumi* Samuel Weiser, New York 1972; a translation of Rumis *Fihi ma fihi*

Arberry, A. J. *An Introduction to the History of Sufism* Longmans, London 1943

Arberry, A. J. *Sufism* 1950; Unwin, London 1979

Armstrong, Karen. *A History of God* 1993; Mandarin Paperbacks, London 1994

Attar, Fariduddin. *The Conference of the Birds*, tr. Afkham Darbandi and Dick Davis Penguin, Harmondsworth 1984

Attar, Fariduddin. *The Conference of the Birds*, tr. C. S. Nott 1954; Routledge & Kegan Paul, London 1978

Attar, Fariduddin. *Muslim Saints and Mystics*, tr. A. J. Arberry 1966; Arkana, London 1990

Bayat, Mojdeh & Jamnia, Mohammad Ali. *Tales from the Land of the Sufis* 1994; Shambhala, Boston 2001

Bayrak, Shaykh Tosun. *The Most Beautiful Names* Threshold Books, Putney, VT 1985

Burckhardt, Titus. *Introduction aux Doctrines ésoteriques de l'Islam* P. Derain, Lyons 1955

Chishti, Shaykh Hakim Moinuddin. *The Book of Sufi Healing* Inner Traditions International, Rochester, VT 1991

Cornell, Rkia. *Early Sufi Women*: Fons Vitae, Louisville KY 1999

Corbin, Henri. *L'Imagination Créatrice dans le Soufisme d'Ibn Arabi*, 2e édition Flammarion, Paris 1975

Cowan, James G. *Where Two Oceans Meet: A Selection of Odes from the Divan of Shems of Tabriz by Mevlana Jalaluddin Rumi* Element Books, Shaftesbury 1992

Danner, Victor. *The Islamic Tradition* Amity House, Warwick, NY 1988

Dermenghem, Émile. *Vies des Saints Musulmans*, Nouvelle Édition: Éditions Baconnier, Algiers n.d.

Ernst, Carl W. trans, *Teachings of Sufism* Shambhala Boston 1999

Haeri, Shaykh Fadhlalla. *The Elements of Islam* Element Books, Shaftesbury 1993

Haeri, Shaykh Fadhlalla. *The Elements of Sufism* Element Books, Shaftesbury 1990

Haeri, Shaykh Fadhlalla. *The Journey of the Self* Element Books, Shaftesbury 1989

Helminski, Camille Adams. *Women of Sufism* Shambhala, Boston 2003

Helminski, Kabir & Algan, Refik *The Drop That Became the Sea* Threshold Books, Putney, VT 1989

Hujwiri. *Kashf al-Mahjub*, tr. R. A. Nicholson 1911; Gibb Memorial Trust, Warminster 2000

Huxley, Aldous. *The Perennial Philosophy* 1946 Triad Grafton, London 1989

Ibn 'Arabi. *Kernel of the Kernel (Lubbu-l-Lubb)* Beshara Publications, Sherborne n.d.

Ibn 'Arabi. *The Seals of Wisdom – From the Fusus al-Hikam* Concord Grove Press, Santa Barbara, CA 1983

Bibliography

Ibn 'Arabi. *Sufis of Andalusia*, tr. R. W. Austin Beshara Publications, Oxford 1988

Ibn 'Arabi. *'Whoso Knoweth Himself . . .* from the *Treatise on Being*, tr. T. H. Weir Beshara Publications, Sherborne 1976

Ibn 'Arabi. *The Wisdom of the Prophets (Fusus al-Hikam)* translated from Arabic to French by Titus Burckhardt, and from French to English by Angela Culme-Seymour Beshara Publications, Aldsworth 1975

Landau, Rom. *The Philosophy of Ibn Arabi* George Allen & Unwin, London 1959

Lings, Martin. *What is Sufism?* (1975; Islamic Texts Society, Cambridge 1993

Macdonald, D. B. *The Religious Life and Attitude in Islam* Chicago, 1909

Nicholson, R. A. *The Mystics of Islam* 1914; Arkana, London 1989

Nicholson, R. A. *Rumi: Poet and Mystic* (1950; Unwin Paperbacks, London: 1978

Nurbaqsh, Dr. Javad. *Sufi Women*: Khaniqahi-Nimatullahi Publications, New York 1990

Ozak, Sheikh Muzaffer. *Love is the Wine*, ed. Sheikh Ragip Frager Threshold Books, Putney, Vermont 1987

Perry, Whitall N. *A Treasury of Traditional Wisdom* Perennial Books, Bedfont 1981

The Persian Mystics: The Invocations of Sheikh 'Abdullah Ansari of Herat, tr. Sardar Sir Jogendra Singh John Murray, London 1939

Pickthall, Marmaduke. *The Meaning of the Glorious Koran: An Explanatory Translation* George Allen & Unwin, London 1930

Rumi, Jalaluddin. *Fihi ma fihi* (see Arberry, *Discourses of Rumi*)

Rumi, Jalaluddin. *The Mathnawi of Jalaluddin Rumi*, ed. and tr. R. A. Nicholson 1930; Gibb Memorial Trust, Cambridge 1982

Schimmel, Annemarie. *Rumi's World* first published as *I Am Wind, You Are Fire*, 1992; Shambhala, Boston 2001

Schuon, Frithjof. *Understanding Islam* World Wisdom Books, 1998

Shabistari. *The Secret Rose Garden*, tr. Florence Lederer n.d.; repr. Phanes Press, Grand Rapids, MI 1987

Shah, Idries. *The Exploits of the Incomparable Mulla Nasrudin* 1966; Picador, London 1978

Shah, Idries. *A Perfumed Scorpion* 1978; Harper & Row, San Francisco 1982

Bibliography

Shah, Idries. *The Sufis* 1964 New York Anchor, 1971

Shah, Idries. *Thinkers of the East* 1971 London Arkana, 1991

Shah, Idries. *The Way of the Sufi* 1968 London Arkana, 1990

Simawna, Shaikh Badruddin of. *Inspirations on the Path of Blame*: A commentary by Shaikh Tosun Bayrak al-Jerrahi al-Halveti Threshold Books, Putney, VT 1993

Smith, Margaret. *Readings from the Mystics of Islam* Luzac, London 1950.

Stoddart, William. *Sufism: The Mystical Doctrines and Methods of Islam* Aquarian Press, Wellingborough 1982

Witteveen, Dr H. J. *Universal Sufism* Element Books, Shaftesbury 1997

Index

Index

Index

Hasan of Basra 89 – 91
heart, symbolism of 20 – 1, 167, 201
heresy 116 – 17, 120, 122
Hermetic tradition 108, 163
'higher self' 9, 143, 195
Hira, Mount 18
Hujwuri *see* Al-Hujwuri
Husamuddin *see* Chelebi, Husamuddin
Husayn, Imam 43, 63, 65

I

Ibn Adham, Ibrahim 66, 95 – 9, 100, 144 – 5
Ibn 'Arabi, Muhyiddin 70, 72, 79, 88, 176
    events of life 162 – 6
    'Perfect Man' concept 167, 170, 171
    on Sufi change 65
    Bezels of Wisdom 167 – 70
    Kernel of the Kernel 170 – 2
    Treatise on Being 172 – 4
Ibn Iyad, Fudayl 103 – 4
Ibn Rushd (Averroes) 163 – 4
intelligence, spiritual 196
intoxicated school 66, 77 – 8, 111, 116, 195, 205 – 7
Isaac 16 – 17
Ishmael 16 – 17, 54 – 5
Islam
    definition 11
    early history 16
    esoteric style 62 – 4, 128
    exoteric style 63 – 4, 69, 128
    fundamental elements of 46 – 8
    influence on architecture 72
    material gains of 90
    oral tradition 32, 46
    reinstatement of *tariqah* 136
    spread of 41, 43 – 4, 66, 88, 90
    and Sufism 10 – 11, 70

J

Jami 68, 190
Jerusalem 15, 23 – 4, 41
Jesus 30, 51
Jews 30
jihad 39
'Joseph and Zulaikha' 80 – 2, 194
Junayd *see* Al-Junayd

K

Ka'ba 16, 21, 23, 33, 40, 47, 51, 54 – 5
Karbala, battle of 43
Kawas, Ibrahim 121
Khadijah (Muhammad's wife) 18, 22, 24
Khan, Hazrat Inayat 72 – 3
Khidr 96, 135, 148, 149, 164
knowledge
    pearls of 202 – 3
    of the Prophet 62
    self-knowledge 188

L

language, transcription of 12, 88
'Layla and Majnun' 82 – 5, 186
Lederer, Florence 201
Lings, Martin 33, 60, 121
love 107, 117, 148 – 9, 154, 155, 178, 181, 201
'lover and the Beloved, the' 79 – 80, 109, 120, 154
'lower self' 9, 71, 143, 152 – 3, 195

M

Majnun *see* 'Layla and Majnun'
Mecca 16, 17, 31, 40, 54, 120, 165
Medina (*formerly* Yathrib) 24 – 5, 31, 39, 89
Messengers 51
Mevlevi Order ('Whirling Dervishes') 69, 175, 179, 180

Index